1985
To add to
your collection!
With love, Anne

The Golden
Age of Flemish
Art

The Golden Age of Flemish Art

William Gaunt

With photographs
by Wim Swaan and others

GREENWICH HOUSE
Distributed by Crown Publishers, Inc.
New York

Fig. 1 *Facing title page*
The Skaters before the Gate of
Saint George at Antwerp;
engraving by Cock after
Pieter Brueghel, 1553.
(9½ x 12in., 24.2 x 30cm.)
London, British Museum

Fig. 2 View of Antwerp
Cathedral from Guicciardini,
published by Plantin, 1581.
Antwerp, Museum Plantin-Moretus.

Copyright © William Gaunt and Paul Elek Productions Limited,
MCMLXIX

This 1983 edition is published by Greenwich House,
a division of Arlington House, Inc, distributed by
Crown Publishers, Inc.

Library of Congress Cataloguing in Publication Data:

Gaunt, William, 1900-
    The Golden Age of Flemish Art.
    (Originally published as *Flemish Cities*)
    Bibliography: p.
    Includes index.
    1. Cities and towns—Flanders. 2. Art—Flanders.
3. Flanders—History, local. I. Swaan, Wim. II. Title.
DH801.F45G34 1983 709'.493'1 83-11713
ISBN 0-517-416468

Printed in Hong Kong by South China Printing Co.

h g f e d c b a

Contents

Acknowledgements

The Publishers would like to thank all those organizations and individuals who co-operated so generously with Mr Swaan during his visit to Belgium to photograph subjects specially for this book. In particular they would like to thank the Burgomaster and Aldermen of Antwerp, Monsieur T. Gerrits of St James, Antwerp, Monsieur Beeckmans of Rubenshuis, Antwerp, Dr L. Voet of the Museum Plantin-Moretus, Antwerp, the Dean of the Cathedral, Brussels, Monsieur Dierinck of Notre-Dame au Sablon, Brussels, Monsieur Jean-Pierre van den Branden of the Maison d'Erasme, Brussels, Kanunnik Valère Laridon of Notre-Dame, Bruges, the Curé of the Cathedral of St Sauveur, Bruges, and Monsieur F. Kesteloot of the Palais de Justice, Bruges.

In addition, the Publishers would like to acknowledge permission to reproduce photographs from the following: Courtesy of the Trustees of the British Museum: plate 8; text illustrations 1, 22, 35, 37, 49; Commissie van Openbaar Onderstand, Bruges: back of the jacket, plates 16, 17, 31, 32, 37, 59; Courtesy of the Trustees of the National Gallery, London: plates 21, 34, 38, 39, 70, 76, 82; text illustrations 19, 38; St Bavon, Ghent: plates 19, 20, 33; Städelsches Kunstinstitut, Frankfurt: plates 23, 24; Metropolitan Museum of Art, New York: plate 22; text illustration 14; Abbaye de Saint-André, Bruges: plate 26; Copyright Bibliothèque Royale de Belgique, Brussels: plates 27, 40; Museo del Prado, Madrid: plates 28, 63, 64, 65, 66; text illustrations 27, 43; Musées Royaux des Beaux Arts de Belgique, Brussels: plates 30, 53, 61, 86; text illustration 9; Copyright A.C.L., Brussels: plates 36, 52, 62, 71, 73, 75; text illustrations 4, 5, 6, 7, 8, 12, 24, 25, 28, 30, 33, 39, 40, 41, 42; Courtesy of the Victoria and Albert Museum, London: plate 67; text illustration 34; Mauritshuis, The Hague: plate 68; Museum Plantin-Moretus, Antwerp: back endpaper; text illustrations 2, 23, 31; Copyright reserved text illustrations 20, 21.

The photographs were provided by the following: Wim Swaan: front endpaper, plates 1, 2, 3, 4, 5, 6, 7, 9, 10, 11, 12, 13, 14, 15, 26, 41, 42, 43, 44, 45, 46, 47, 48, 49, 50, 51, 55, 56, 57, 67, 69, 78, 80, 84, 85, 87, 88, 89, 90, 92, 93; text illustrations 26, 36, 47, 48, 50, 51; John R. Freeman, London: plate 8; text illustrations 22, 35, 37, 49; Louis Loose, Brussels: back of the jacket, plates 16, 31; Scala, Florence: plates 18, 19, 20, 60, 63, 64, 65, 66, 91, 94, 95; Joachim Blaüel, Munich: plates 23, 24; Giraudon, Paris: plates 25, 54, 96; Paul Bijtebier, Brussels: plates 33, 72, 74, 77; text illustrations 11, 13, 29; Service de Documentation Photographique de la Réunion des Musées Nationaux, Versailles: plates 29, 58; J. T'. Felt, Antwerp: text illustrations 2, 23, 31; Bulloz, Paris: text illustrations 15, 17; Carlton Studios, London: text illustration 34.

List of plates

8

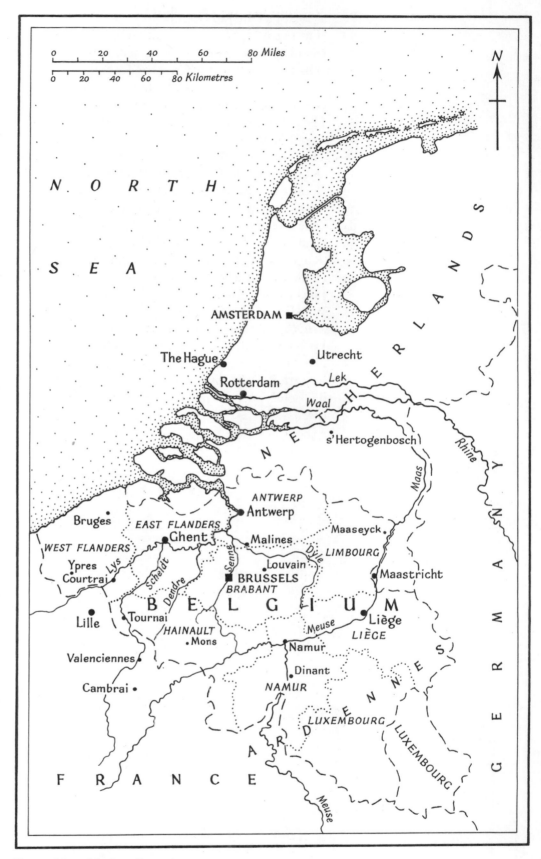

Fig. 3   Map of the Low Countries.

The Gothic Splendour

It is the historic glory of the cities of the southern Netherlands, from the Middle Ages to the 17th century, to have been great centres of the arts. They brought architecture, sculpture, painting, manuscript illumination and decorative craft into related magnificence. Above all they fostered a pictorial art that is one of the supreme European achievements and legacies. The development is an aesthetic drama in three acts; first of medieval growth that reached its zenith of late-Gothic splendour in the 15th century, then a disturbed but still creative period of transition, followed at last by a second golden age, the age of Rubens.

The height reached in the first great period is superbly exemplified in the city of Bruges. As in the painting of some 15th-century master it may be imagined then as the perfected type of medieval city, such a place as William Morris loved to dream of, enclosed by picturesque walls and gates, its towers and spires piercing the sky in Gothic harmony, the churches, market halls and mansions of patrician and wealthy bourgeois, presided over by the wonderful belfry (with its famous chimes) that was already 200 years old.

In the 15th century, Bruges had already passed the peak of the commercial and industrial prosperity it had long enjoyed. By 1400, the river Zwijn, its lifeline to the sea and the sea-borne trade that had brought it so much wealth, had already begun to silt up. Yet the English mariners, as familiar with the river's course as with the reaches of the Thames, were still able to negotiate it, bringing the fine wool for which England was noted and returning home with the woven stuffs of Bruges, with French wines and the spices and exotic products for which the city was the entrepôt.

Bruges was also at this time the centre of a great commercial system, an international seat of monetary exchange, a headquarters of the Hanseatic League, its operations stretching from the Baltic to the Adriatic Sea. A proud self-governing Commune, ruled by mayor and aldermen, with its powerful guilds of wool merchants, linen merchants, mercers and brewers and fifty-two guilds of craftsmen, in this century it formed part of the rich Burgundian domain. The Dukes of Burgundy brought a new element of luxury and colour into life and gave an immense stimulus to the arts. Their example as patrons was followed by the aristocratic Seigneurs of the Gruuthuse, by such capitalists as Peter Bladelin, treasurer of the Golden Fleece.

It was characteristic of Burgundy to have invested wool, the source of democratic wealth, with chivalrous prestige in this order of knighthood, instituted by Philip the Good on his marriage to Isabella of Portugal in 1429. Jehan Puetin, goldsmith of Bruges, fashioned for a knight of the Order a most elaborate ceremonial collar of gold and enamel, its emblem wrought in solid gold.

The sober garb of the merchants from all parts of Europe who thronged the Grand'Place was diversified by the extravagance of courtly dress, and business dealings round the market hall by sumptuous open-air entertainments. Young John Paston, among the English company which arrived for the wedding of Margaret of York with Duke Charles the Bold in 1469, was dazzled by the richness of attire, the cloth of gold and tapestries that lined the glittering processional route, and could think of nothing like it 'save King Arthur's Court'.

Painting enjoyed an unprecedented favour – with the Burgundians, connoisseurs especially of the manuscript book and its miniatures (an art practised at Bruges since the 13th century) – with the wealthy burgesses whose pride it was to give an altarpiece to some religious foundation – with the foreign merchants and agents who were frequent clients for portraiture. At the annual fairs, paintings and miniatures were among the most popular of the varied products offered for sale. It is not to be wondered at that Bruges in the 15th century had become a magnet attracting artists from far and wide.

In the heyday thus outlined, contemporary observers such as Adrien Barland of Louvain conceded that Bruges outshone the other cities of Flanders, Hainault and Brabant, beautiful as Ghent, Antwerp, Brussels, Louvain and Malines might be. Yet other cities also had their special distinction in the arts, their special prestige from the masters who came to work there. They had a parallel evolution within the limits of the 'Low Countries' or Netherlands in the wider sense, comprising the present-day Holland, Belgium and the Duchy of Luxembourg.

Geographically and internally the Netherlands as a whole formed a coherent region, a plain of uninterrupted extent from Holland to Flanders, bounded to the East by the forests and rocky uplands of the Ardennes and by the river Meuse. It was never a single state, however. The cities grew in the post-Carolingian epoch in the territories arbitrarily parcelled out between feudal lords, lay and ecclesiastical. The vague *imperium* of the Germanic Empire was represented by the Bishoprics of Liège and Cambrai, the Counties of Namur, Luxembourg, Limbourg and Holland. From the 9th century the land to the west of the Scheldt was ruled by the Counts of Flanders who owed allegiance to the King of France.

In the flat lands traversed by the Scheldt and its tributaries the townships that revived or came into being after the depredations of the Norsemen in the 9th century gained an early economic advantage. Near the castles built to withstand the invader, merchants were allowed to set up their trading stations and hold their periodic fairs. At an early date they began the manufacture of woollen cloth that was to become a main source of wealth. In the 10th century the feudal overlord, Count Baldwin III of Flanders, approved a weaving and dyeing industry at Ghent. From the 11th century wool was woven into cloth and marketed at Bruges, Ghent, Lille, Arras, Ypres and Douai. It was exported to England, France, Germany and Italy. Geographically, the cities of Flanders had a double advantage in being well placed for the revival of commerce between North and South in Europe and in access to the North Sea – as vital to medieval Bruges as the Adriatic to Venice.

Born or reborn in the age of castle and monastery, the cities provided an alternative to the self-contained manorial system and a purely monastic culture. Free of feudal ties save for the dues paid to the titular ruler, they formed merchant and craft guilds with their own obligations and rights and recognized a democratic, or oligarchic, authority in the persons of the mayor and aldermen who administered justice and civic affairs. As the settlements prospered they were enclosed with walls of stone (which the Ardennes region supplied). The castle which had given protection was incorporated within them.

A tremendous relic, like a great rock round which the city has grown, is the Castle of the Counts of Flanders at Ghent (see plate 1). Unlike the castle at Bruges which was demolished in the 15th century and the 'Steen' at Antwerp which remains only as a fragment, it has lasted through the centuries and been restored in modern times to all its stern original majesty. The phases of civic history are implicit in its structure. The cellars of the *donjon* go back to the 9th century when the first Count of Flanders, Baldwin of the Iron Arm, built his fortress in defence against the raiding Norsemen. The castle that replaced it in 1180 is perhaps the most impressive Romanesque stronghold in Europe, apparently designed as much to awe the populace as to guard against invaders.

The medieval growth of the cities is marked by the outward extension of their encircling walls. From its first island circumference, indicated by the course of the Dyver and the Roya, Bruges expanded within ramparts nearly five miles round. The walls of Brussels required a similar extension in the 14th century, remaining substantially intact until the early 19th century. The evolution of 'Gothic' architecture gives a remarkable commentary on the evolution of the country, influenced as it was by both the feudal constitution of the Netherlands and their geographical place between Germany and France. Germany was slow to adopt the elegance of pointed arch and traceried window, the soaring grace typical of Gothic construction, preferring the simplicity and massiveness of the Romanesque style that preceded it. France from the 12th century took the lead in the creation of characteristic Gothic forms. The influence of both countries is to be seen in the Netherlands, the northern regions favouring the German simplicity, the South drawing inspiration from the Gothic churches of the Ile-de-France. The difference between the various ecclesiastical styles of the Middle Ages is further explained by the separate allegiance of the Netherlandish bishoprics, those of Utrecht and Liège to Cologne and of Arras, Cambrai and Tournai to Rheims.

Fig. 4　Detail of the Bruges belfry from 'The Life of Saint Lucy' by the Master of the Legend of Saint Lucy, c. 1480. *Bruges, Saint Jacques.*

The great churches of the southern Netherlands show a mingling of style, as in the striking contrast presented by the 12th–13th-century cathedral of Tournai, between Romanesque nave and towers and the Gothic elegance of the choir. St Gudule, Brussels, in its imposing west front combines the northern plainness with fully developed Gothic features. The cathedral church of St Sauveur at Bruges bears the stamp of many periods and the massive brick west tower, the lower part of which dates from the 12th century, proclaims its affiliation with the Germanic Romanesque.

The most original developments in architecture were the secular Gothic buildings that expressed the independent character and pride of the southern cities and their mercantile prosperity of the 13th and 14th centuries, and also, during the last phase of Gothic, the flamboyant style of the 15th century. In the early Middle Ages the city itself had become a stronghold, with a timber watchtower instead of a castle keep, elaborated in the course of time into that distinctive feature of Flanders, Hainault and Artois, the belfry. Unique in several ways, the belfry of the southern Netherlands is a reminder of a fevered political history, of incessant conflict, which was the reverse side of the fruitful contact with neighbouring lands in the arts. After the Crusades and the fantastic adventure so sardonically described by Gibbon which made Count Baldwin IX of Flanders and Hainault the ruler of Constantinople, his own land, weakly governed, became the prey of France. The 14th century was a time of continual turmoil, of French conquest and Flemish insurrection, of fierce rivalries between the cities, of civic strife between the proletarian workers and the wealthy bourgeois, of the difficulties produced by the Hundred Years War between France and England.

The belfry then had a vital function. A lofty tower, it enabled watch to be kept over a wide area of the surrounding plain against the approach of enemy forces. Its bells pealed the alarm, roused the forces of law and order when the workers of Ghent rebelled against their industrial masters in 1302 and massacred mayor and aldermen; summoned the Flemish burghers to arms when the master-weaver of Bruges, Peter de Conyne, led them to victory against the French at the battle of Courtrai; conveyed the news of the demagogue Jacob van Artevelde's murder and in 1382 of the death of his son, Philip, in battle against the French at Rosebeke.

The belfry was a multi-purpose building. Below ground level were prison cells and the torture chamber with its medieval equipment of chains, racks and branding-irons. Above was the court room where prior to the building of a separate town hall, the mayor and aldermen met and sat in judgment. There would be a guard room also for the sentinels of the tower, an arsenal of weapons, a municipal treasury with iron-bound coffers, moored to wall and floor and fitted with elaborate locks, containing specie, objects of special value, official records and seals. Other features were an open balcony from which proclamations were read and a weather-vane, often shaped in grotesque animal form, like the copper dragon at Ghent fancifully supposed to have been brought back by the Crusaders from Constantinople. Looted from Bruges in 1382 for the belfry of Ghent it was one of the most celebrated of the symbols that took the shape of a tutelary demon.

The importance of the belfry was also great in the peaceful periods of city life. In the normal course it regulated the community's hours of work and play. Until the use of clocks in the 14th century, the hours were marked by a trumpet-call from the tower, followed by a spoken announcement of the time through a megaphone, a sun-dial being an addition to the façade. From the 15th century the invention of the chiming-clock replaced hand-ringing. Memory of the human bell-ringers was preserved in the mechanical figures which came into use to strike the hour. Special carillons also accompanied the pageant entry of visitors of state and other occasions of ceremony and fête. Often they were supplemented by a concert of musicians stationed in the tower. The quality and intricate melodies of the carillons at Bruges, Ghent, Ypres and Tournai were renowned. In design the belfry transcended function. The tallest belfry in Belgium, that of Bruges, over 350 feet high, is a beautiful construction in the brick which gives so many attractions to the city's architecture (see plate 8). Begun in 1280 when fire had destroyed the original wooden watch-tower, it remains substantially one of the supreme Gothic wonders.

The market hall or cloth hall was the great architectural development of the 13th and 14th centuries, called for by the amazing growth of the weaving industry and the cloth trade. The *Halle* served as a communal warehouse, market and meeting place for the merchants and their many international clients. Although other commodities might be dealt with, including wine, oil and spices (so highly valued in the Middle Ages) the greater part of the space was given over to textiles. The *Halle* essentially consisted of a vast ground floor, with two or three aisles and stalls where the merchants displayed their wares, under the strict rules of the guild which restrained them from competition openly conducted, and which required that the quality of cloth should be uniformly high. The material, after official examination, was literally stamped with a seal of approval.

The Cloth Hall at Ypres, a leading marketing centre, was the most imposing of these magnificent commercial buildings. Built between 1200 and 1304, to a plan as simple as it was grand, with a long, symmetrical row of windows and a dominant central tower, it was a masterpiece of secular Gothic. Its destruction with the rest of the city in the incessant bombardments of the First World War was a dire reminder of the invasion hazard to which Belgium throughout history has been exposed. If lacking something of architectural life, the reconstruction since made still conveys its grandeur.

Churches and public buildings in any country commonly display the workmanship of different periods. In the Gothic Netherlands this is even more often the case than elsewhere. Differences of style in the same building were often due to the ups and downs of political and economic circumstances which made building activity intermittent, stopping and resumed when conditions allowed, perhaps after a considerable lapse of time. The tower of the church of Notre-Dame at Bruges (see plate 5) dates from 1297, but its outer aisles were built in the 14th and 15th centuries; in the 15th century also the beautiful 'Paradise Porch' was added in late-Gothic style. Tall as it is the belfry of Ghent never reached its intended height. The decline of the cloth industry is signalized by Ghent's Cloth Hall, one of the last buildings of its kind, constructed at the foot of the belfry between 1425 and 1441 but never finished.

Yet the same period marks the end of many distresses of the feudal era, a return to settled conditions, the advent of a new age of luxury in which the symptoms of commercial decay were cloaked from view, and a great efflorescence of all the arts. The union of Flanders with the dukedom of Burgundy, of key importance in contributing to these results, was foreshadowed by the marriage of Philip the Bold with Marguerite, daughter of the Count of Flanders, Louis de Maele, in 1369. After Louis' death in 1384 the new Burgundian dominion became a corridor thrust across Europe as well as a counter to the pre-eminence of France, giving Flanders the protection it needed and making it decisively the European centre in art.

The France of the Valois kings, with a powerful rival on the flank, and a demented monarch, Charles VI, on the throne, who had been crushingly defeated by the English at Agincourt in 1415, was no longer the influence or the threat it had been. Philip the Bold was determined to excel Paris in the magnificence of his court at Dijon. His brother and rival connoisseur, Jean, Duke of Berry, sought a like magnificence in his court at Bourges. The stone carvers, painters and illuminators of the Netherlands were in demand with both, as well as artists from France.

Philip's grandson, Philip the Good, who ruled from 1419 to 1467 was no less a devotee of all that was luxurious, the patron of musicians, poets and painters, delighting in costly entertainments, rich embroideries and the extravagances of fashion in which Burgundy took the lead. In architecture the evolution of the Gothic style, increasingly tending to rich embellishment, intricacy of carving and the flame-like tracery known as 'flamboyant', matched the general love of luxury. Building with much decorative ornament was a passion of the 15th century, shared equally by the nobles and the burghers. It was the century of the *Hôtel de Ville*, intended to provide more suitable premises for the civic authorities than the market hall and a place of fitting majesty for any important occasion.

The exterior of the typical *Hôtel de Ville* was lavishly decorated with carved ornament and sculptured figures. It generally consisted of two storeys, the lower being given over to the kitchens and various offices, the upper storey containing the large and richly appointed aldermanic chamber, adorned with wall paintings and sculptured detail and having a large and ornate chimney-piece. This was the scene of banquets, balls, theatrical entertainments and municipal elections. The first of these celebrated town halls was that of Bruges (see plate 9), a graceful example of Gothic, recalling the Sainte-Chapelle of Paris and begun in 1376. Its steep roof, pierced by dormer windows and flanked by pinnacles, its traceried windows originally filled with stained glass, its façade enriched with sculptured niches, foretold the luxurious character of such later town halls as those of Brussels (1401–55) (see plate 7), Louvain (1448) and Audenarde (1525) in which the cities vied in the assertion of civic dignity.

Flamboyant Gothic left a strong imprint on the Flemish cities. Its complex curves appear in the upper storey of the Chapelle du Saint Sang at Bruges (Chapel of the Holy Blood, see plate 15), in striking contrast with the lower storey of this miniature church, perhaps the oldest building in the city, dating back to the 12th century. Many a flamboyant porch or mansion gateway is depicted in delightful detail by the Netherlandish masters of painting. In close association with archi-

Fig. 5 Detail from the Altar of Saint George by Jan Borman the Elder. *Brussels, Musées Royaux d'Art et d'Histoire.*

tecture was the development of sculpture and the related crafts. Their history, together with that of painting in the same period illuminates the fact that every part of the Netherlands made a contribution to the genius of the Gothic age; and that the Burgundian connoisseurs did much to encourage the movement of artists from place to place, this also making for a great synthesis of talent.

There was a long tradition of craft. By the 12th century goldsmithing flourished in the Meuse valley, under the patronage of the archbishops of Cologne. The goldsmiths produced shrines and reliquaries fashioned like ecclesiastical buildings, covered with gold and decorated with enamel and representations of figures along the arcaded sides. The skill of the Meuse goldsmith, Nicholas of Verdun, whose works were exported to Germany set a style that was long followed there. In the 13th and 14th centuries there was a flourishing school of Franco-Flemish sculpture and it was in this period also that the altarpiece carved in wood began to appear. A realistic sense of three dimensions was a development of the late 14th century, represented by the work of André Beauneveu, probably born at Valenciennes, sculptor and miniature painter, who worked at Ypres, Malines, at the court of Charles V of France and also for the Duke of Berry at Bourges. When Philip the Bold sought craftsmen for Dijon he had a wealth of Netherlandish talent upon which to draw. Outstanding was the Dutch sculptor, Claus Sluter, born at Haarlem, who is first mentioned as a member of the stone-carvers' guild at Brussels in 1379, whence he was invited by Philip the Bold to work at the Carthusian monastery of Champmol, near Dijon.

The clashes of religion that were still in the future, the iconoclastic outbursts that were later to destroy a large amount of Gothic sculpture in the Netherlands, have left its history fragmentary. So little remains in the North that sculpture is scarcely associated with Holland and it comes as a surprise that such a sculptor as Sluter, whose greatness is still revealed in the dignified realism of the figures he carved for the Champmol Chartreuse and the tomb of Philip the Bold (see plate 54) should have been Dutch by origin. He seems to emerge from a school of sculptors in the South, the nature of which is suggested by the carved corbels of prophets from the portal of the old Town Hall in Brussels (Musée Communal) and the corbels from the Town Hall of Bruges (Gruuthuse Museum, Bruges) by Jean de Valenciennes, 1379–80, illustrating the story of Tristan and Isolde (see figs. 6 & 8).

Sluter, who died in the winter of 1405–6 represents – and no doubt by his example encouraged – the continuance of a tradition of monumental stone-carving. In the course of the 15th century however sculpture took several distinctive forms. Funerary sculpture was a great development of the southern Netherlands. There are such examples as the bronze tomb of Joan and William I of Brabant in the Carmelite church in Brussels, commissioned in 1458 by Philip the Good and carried

Fig. 6   Two carved corbels showing 'The Prophets' from the portal of the old Town Hall, Brussels. *Brussels, Musée Communal.*

Fig. 7   Bronze effigy of Isabella of Bourbon, reputed to be by Jacques de Gérines and Renier van Thienen. *Antwerp, the Cathedral.*

Fig. 8 Corbel from the town hall of Bruges, by Jean de Valenciennes, illustrating the story of Tristan and Isolde. *Bruges, Gruuthusemuseum.*

Fig. 9 Altar of the Passion made for the Italian merchant and donor, Claudio de Villa, in about 1470. *Brussels, Musées Royaux des Beaux Arts.*

out by a sculptor of Tournai and the Brussels brassfounder, Jacques de Gérines; the recumbent bronze effigy of Isabella of Bourbon (1476) now in Antwerp Cathedral, also perhaps the work of Gérines and his successor at Brussels, Renier van Thienen, a masterpiece of rhythmic design; and the beautiful monument to the Duchess Mary of Burgundy, cast in bronze from a wooden model by the master wood-carver, Jan Borman, in the van Thienen foundry (1491–8). This exquisite work, so sensitive and free from formal convention, emanates serenity in the church of Notre-Dame at Bruges (see plate 53).

The art in which Borman also excelled was that of the carved altarpiece, the narrative and highly detailed form of sculpture in which the 15th century was prolific. Many were produced in Brussels, Antwerp, Malines and Liège. They were famous throughout Europe and exported in quantity to France, Germany, Sweden and Spain, bearing (as textiles did) a stamp that identified and guaranteed the workmanship. The altarpiece was a meeting-point of the arts; Gothic architecture provided its framework. The Altar of the Passion made in Brussels in about 1470 for an Italian merchant and donor, Claudio de Villa (Musées Royaux, Brussels), reproduces flamboyant intricacy in the arches surmounting its three panels and the background of the scene of Crucifixion. Spirited action on a Gothic stage, overhung by an arcading of elaborate tracery, is strikingly exemplified in the Altar of St George by Jan Borman the Elder (1493), originally at Louvain and now in the Musée du Cinquantenaire at Brussels (see plate 52 & fig. 5).

The sculpture was habitually painted and gilded and thus called for the collaboration of master-painters as *polychromeurs*. When Philip the Bold, on a tour through his Flemish domain in 1390, selected Jacques de Baerze, wood-carver at Termonde near Bruges, to make altarpieces for Champmol, he assigned the task of gilding and painting and providing painted wings to his court painter, Melchior Broederlam of Ypres.

The greatest masters of the century, not excluding Jan van Eyck and Roger van der Weyden, were employed on this subsidiary task. The arts of sculptor, goldsmith and colourist were combined in the reliquaries that contained the objects of medieval veneration. The reliquary of Charles the Bold fashioned by the Lille goldsmith, Gérard Loyet (1467), now in the Diocesan Museum, Liège, portrays in three dimensions the kneeling Duke (with the crystal prism that contained the supposed finger of St Lambert) and St George with the dragon slain at his feet. Gold and enamel enrich their panoply of armour. The most famous object of the kind is the Shrine of St Ursula in the Hôpital St Jean (Hospital of St John) at Bruges, completed in 1489 when the Bishop of Bruges placed in it the relics of the saint which it had been designed to contain (see plate 16). The painted ornamentation of this Gothic chapel in gilded miniature, the tour-de-force of Hans Memlinc, brilliantly wedded the Bruges miniature style with the architecture of this remarkable casket, in illustration of the legendary wanderings of St Ursula and her cohort of virgins and their massacre at Cologne.

The supreme expression of the Netherlandish genius in the late Gothic age was in painting. As in any great period of art it presents a fascinating complexity of sources, influences and characteristics. Woven into its texture are medieval piety, the democratic realism of the Flemish cities, the elegant refinement of royal and ducal courts. Art was no longer the prerogative of the monasteries, and painters were craftsmen of the town, linked as all craftsmen were in guilds: the painters' guild of St Luke who, tradition had it, had portrayed the Virgin, or the illuminators' guild of St John. They travelled freely in the Netherlands, North and South, becoming affiliated to guilds other than those of their own cities or working for some art-loving prince as 'varlet de chambre', 'escrivain' or 'enlumineur'. No barrier as yet of religion, no existing opposition of politics between one dominion and another restricted this freedom of movement. France and the Flemish cities might be bitterly at odds in the 14th century but this did not prevent Pierre de Bruxelles, Jean de Gand, Evrard de Hainault and other Flemish miniaturists from working for the court at Paris together with French colleagues.

The Franco-Flemish miniature of the 14th century and the opening years of the 15th century is a last refinement of feudalism, an awakening of interest in nature, a herald, together with the first tentative essays in the altarpiece, of the great school of painting to come. These are elements in the incomparable work, the *Très Riches Heures* (Musée Condé, Chantilly) produced for Jean, Duke of Berry by the brothers, Pol, Jeannequin and Herman of Limbourg (a region fertile in talent) with some collaboration from André de Beauneveu and Jacquemart de Hesdin, also Flemish protégés of the Duke (see plate 25).

The artists were his intimates, housed in luxury at Bourges, heaped with gifts of money and jewels. They repaid him with a masterpiece in which the grandeur of his possessions was depicted in veracious detail, the tapestries of his banqueting hall, identifiable by their mention in inventories, the great salt that adorned his table, his palace in Paris, the châteaux at Vincennes, Riom, Etampes, Poitiers, where he had vast estates. The calendar is already a repertoire of landscape such as the Flemish painters would later cultivate. The joy of spring is conveyed in the flower-spangled meadow that is the setting for a noble cavalcade. The round of peasant labour in winter, summer and autumn is an idyll painted with a sophisticated delicacy – giving no hint of the cruelty and extortions of the Duke who savagely crushed the peasant rising of *Tuchins* and *Cochins* and fought as fiercely against the burghers of the Flemish cities at the battle of Rosebeke.

In such a delicious hybrid as the *Très Riches Heures* of around 1411, half elegantly French and half realistically Flemish in its observation of nature and daily life, the art of the manuscript painter advances towards the more specifically Flemish and Burgundian art of the 15th century so greatly encouraged by that lover of the *de luxe* manuscript book, Philip the Good. He is the receiver of countless pictorial dedications, and the magnificent Burgundian Library preserved in the Bibliothèque Royale at Brussels contains a number of them. Wearing the long black robe of Burgundian court dress (the last word in fashion in an age of colour) and the collar of the Golden Fleece, he receives the copy of *Le Champion des Dames* from the kneeling scribe, Martin le Franc. In dandified attire, his hat of huge dimensions tied with a scarf beneath his chin, with pleated coat, tight hose and pointed shoes, he accepts the *Livre du Gouvernement des Princes* written at Mons in 1452 (see also fig. 10).

The production of these illustrated manuscript books was now localized in and distributed among the cities, Bruges, Ghent, Brussels, Mons, Valenciennes, Hesdin, Lille, Audenarde. Artists who would once have gone to Paris now went to these centres where it is possible to speak of publishing houses in quite a modern sense and for which whole *ateliers* of miniature painters worked. Discrimination against

Fig. 10 Chronicles of Hainault by Jean Wauquelin; fifteenth century. Dedicatory frontispiece showing Philip the Good and his councillors. *Brussels, Bibliothèque Royale.*

the sale of books produced in Holland which was enforced at Bruges caused a number of Dutch artists, such as Guillaume Vrelant to move to the Flemish city and operate as its citizens. The output of the publishing houses reflects the secular direction of the patrons' interests, being no longer confined to missals and books of hours but having a wide literary scope. Histories and chronicles, romances, translations of Aristotle, Xenophon, Petrarch, treatises on various subjects, occupied such publishers, scribes and literary editors as David Aubert at Bruges and Jean Wauquelin at Mons. Besides the copies *de grand luxe* for noble bibliophiles, modest versions of the same works were produced for middle-class buyers.

A celebrated production of Wauquelin was the *Chroniques de Hainault* for which a number of artists supplied miniatures (Bibliothèque Royale, Brussels), the dedicatory frontispiece to Philip the Good being exceptionally fine and in itself a gallery of 15th-century portraits (see fig. 10). Simon Marmion born at Amiens, who settled at Valenciennes in 1458 and earned the title of 'prince of illuminators' is noted especially for the *Pontifical de L'Eglise de Sens* (Bibliothèque Royale, Brussels) with its beautiful, if mannered, painting of the Crucifixion (see plate 27).

The masterpiece of Jean Le Tavernier who settled at Audenarde and worked for Philip the Good was the *Chroniques de Charlemagne* (Bibliothèque Royale, Brussels) with its 105 miniatures, 1458–60, including a fascinating glimpse of a Flemish town and its gateway (bearing the arms of Burgundy), executed in grisaille (see plate 40). At Brussels there was Dreux Jean who illustrated a work of piety for Margaret of York with a composition in which a faithful rendering of St Gudule Cathedral appears and the church of the Sablon in the background. Important at Bruges were the Utrecht painter, Vrelant and his compatriot Loyset Liédet. A number of works produced for the local Maecenas, Louis de Gruuthuse, were illuminated by the Ghent painter, Liévin van Lathem, among them a sumptuous *History of the Golden Fleece* (Bibliothèque Nationale, Paris). At Ghent in the second half of the 15th century, where the industrious publisher-scribe David Aubert was also active, many devotional manuscripts were produced for Margaret of York, wife of Charles the Bold, illuminated by the anonymous 'Master of Mary of Burgundy'.

Though style naturally varied from city to city and artist to artist there are certain characteristics that generally reappear in all the brilliant manuscript art of the 15th century. The decorative border is elaborate, no longer a convention of ivy and vine leaf but introducing different flowers and plants as well as birds and animals among the curves of acanthus which the French miniature had freely adapted from Italy. Realism towards the end of the century revolutionized the border, discarding decoration and giving to flowers, butterflies and insects the *trompe l'œil* appearance of actual objects strewn on the parchment. The Master of Mary of Burgundy made this original innovation. The same treatment appears in the celebrated manuscript produced at Bruges, the Grimani Breviary (Library of St Mark, Venice). The enchanting product of the Flemish miniature painter with its distances of landscape, and sometimes of sea and ships, its slices of life, observant and contemporary in the depiction of modes and manners, however antique or fabulous the subject, and with its use of Gothic architecture as an exterior or interior setting is of course closely related to the art of the panel painter on his larger scale. The two types of work ran a parallel course in the 15th century and as the same artists often practised both it is the easier to understand the connection between them.

Yet a profound difference was to declare itself between the Burgundian art of the book and the Netherlandish painting of which Jan van Eyck was the first great master, with some (still indistinct) collaboration from his elder brother, Hubert.

1   The Castle of the Counts of Flanders, Ghent.

2   Hôpital Saint Jean; the old entrance from the water, Bruges.

3   Quai aux Herbes, Bruges.

4   Quai aux Herbes, Ghent.

26

28

MARIA ERGO ACCEPIT LIBRAM VNGETI NARDI PISTICI PҴIOSE ET VXIT PEDES IħV

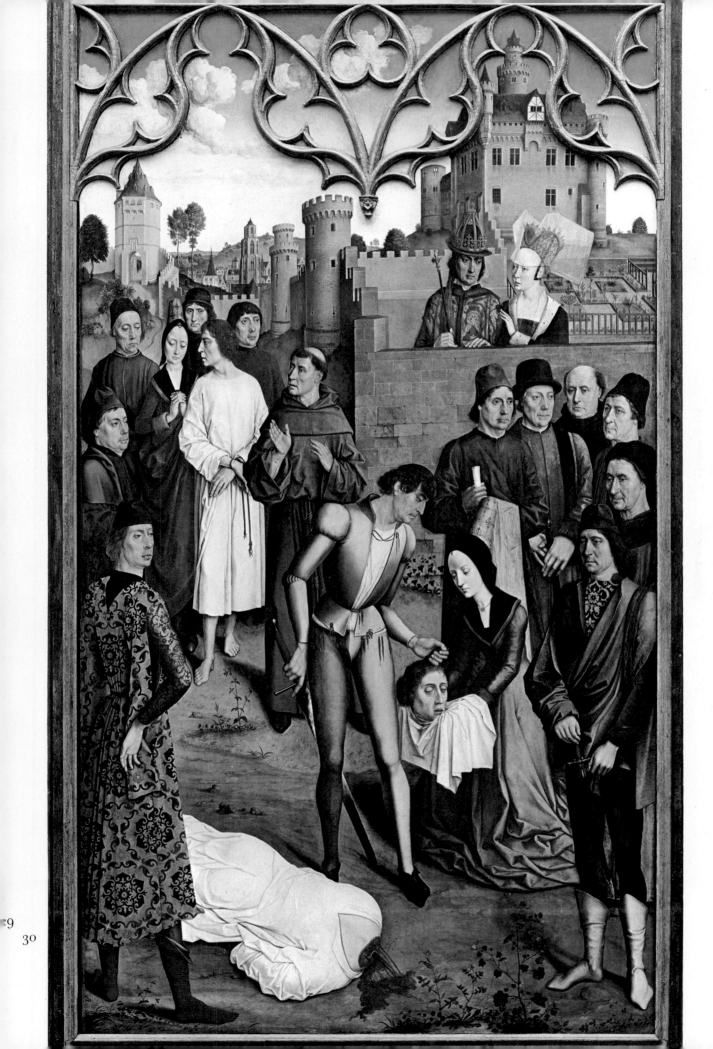

Fig. 11   Detail from 'The Adoration of the Lamb', when closed, showing a portrait of the donor, Joos Vijt, in prayer, executed in monochrome. *Ghent, Saint Bavon.*

5   Spire of the Church of Notre-Dame and old gabled houses, Bruges.

6   The north tower of the cathedral, Antwerp.

7   Hôtel de Ville and Grand'Place, Brussels.

'International Gothic', the term nowadays used to define certain characteristics common to painting in Europe from about 1370 to 1420, ceases to apply. International Gothic was the current of sophisticated and courtly elegance in colour and pattern that creates a certain link between the work of the brothers Limbourg, of Simone Martini, Gentile da Fabriano and Pisanello in Italy, of Stephan Lochner in Germany, of Ferrer Bassa and others in Spain. It was, however, an art of decorative surface, not probing deeply either into character or the material reality of things. The sense of character and the richness of aesthetic significance in material realities were by contrast the special qualities that mark the achievement of the Netherlandish masters. They express a national genius, that of the Netherlands as a whole, and gave to painting an originality that commanded the admiration of all Europe, even of Renaissance Italy and had an influence extending from France and Germany to Italy, Spain and Portugal.

The close connection between the different arts is to be seen in the development of this wonderful school. It is only in part accurate to say that it evolved from the practice of the miniaturist. If the fineness of detail was transferred from the vellum page to the smooth gesso-surfaced wood panel, sculpture also was an inspiring force. The carved and painted altarpiece in three dimensions was a prototype for the painter suggesting how he might give the effect of space on his flat panel. Gothic sculpture was consciously imitated in the grey stone-like monotone of grisaille with which it became usual to depict figures on the outside of an altarpiece's inner wings, and which can be seen when they are closed (see fig. 11). It would be reasonable to suppose that the sharp cuts of the sculptor's chisel suggested the angular folds of drapery that became characteristic of painting, though there seems to have been an interaction, a mutually fructifying effect. For instance, the Dutch sculptor Nikolaus Gerhaert of Leyden (*c.* 1425–73) seems to have carried to Germany and Austria, where his influence was mainly felt, a strongly defined system of folds derived from his acquaintance with the painting of van Eyck. It is possible that the calm, humanist dignity of the sculpture of Claus Sluter on the other hand, which gave to the figures of religious imagining so entirely human an aspect, aroused a kindred feeling in painters who, like Jan van Eyck, depicted bygone saints and living donors equally as creatures of flesh and blood.

Religious painting, recalling the great part that religion played in medieval life even though art was no longer exclusively ruled by churchmen, had a secular element distinct from the luxurious ministration to the pride of a court. The painters it is true were employed by the Burgundian dukes, but they had an independent practice which allied them with the self-made men, the financiers, capitalists, captains of medieval industry and others who affirmed both their dutiful piety and social status by commissioning an altarpiece in which they themselves would be portrayed. The essentially national character of the school is reinforced by the Netherlandish types it inimitably depicts.

It remains surprising that the apparently sudden new departure and magnificent achievement represented by the painting of the van Eycks should have come about. It may be contrasted with a panel painting of the Crucifixion with St Catherine and St Barbara by an anonymous artist, probably of Bruges, in St Sauveur at Bruges (see fig. 12). This was painted about the year 1400 with a frail linear delicacy of style that indicates some acquaintance with the art of Siena. How extraordinary the difference in mature style and power in the 'Adoration of the Lamb' at Ghent, attributed to both the brothers van Eyck and painted little more than thirty years later! The fair amount that is known of Jan van Eyck's career is informative about a 15th-century painter's movements, duties and privileges. There is reason to suppose that he was born at Maaseyck, near Maastricht, in that eastern province of Limbourg that had already been so fruitful of genius. It is known that he made a bequest to Maaseyck and that his daughter eventually entered a convent there. After an apprenticeship, most likely in the Maastricht-Cologne area, he embarked on the travels and the kind of service that were typical of the age. He is first located at the Hague where he worked between 1422 and 1425 for John of Bavaria, Count of Holland, as the latter's disbursements testify. There is some reason to think that his activities included additions to a Book of Hours begun for the Count's predecessor, William IV. In surviving fragments of this manuscript, long preserved at Turin

Fig. 12   Crucifixion, with Saint Catherine and Saint Barbara; anonymous painting c. 1400. *Bruges, Saint Sauveur.*

but mostly destroyed by fire in 1904, the van Eyck manner has been discerned. After the death of John of Bavaria in 1425 he was promptly welcomed by Philip the Good to the Burgundian realm, appointed court painter and 'varlet de chambre' and set up in a house at Lille where he lived for two years.

Like Rubens at a later time he had a part in affairs of state. He became a confidant and intimate of the Duke (who acted as godfather to his first child) and was sent on a number of diplomatic and secret journeys abroad including visits to Portugal and Spain. He settled at Bruges in 1431 and had such official employment as painting and gilding statues of the Counts and Countesses for the new town hall. Though the Duke seems to have subsidized him handsomely he evidently retained independence as a painter. He painted altarpieces to the commission of various wealthy donors and portraits, some evidently for his own satisfaction, like that of his wife, Margareta (Groeningemuseum, Bruges, see fig. 13).

Speculation has never ceased to envelop the enigmatic figure of Jan van Eyck's brother, Hubert. It might be presumed they worked together at the Hague and came southwards at the same time. There are references to the painter, Hubert, in various spellings of the name, in the records of Ghent, that indicate his having settled and painted there. He died at Ghent in 1426 and was buried in the precincts of the cathedral of St Bavon. The lapidary museum in the remains of the abbey of St Bavon contains his tombstone found during the restoration of the cathedral in 1892. Jan van Eyck is so distinct in a series of signed and dated paintings that the absence of any such by Hubert makes him the more mysterious. Much debated still is the latter's part in the great altarpiece, 'The Adoration of the Lamb' (see plates 18, 19 & 33), given to the cathedral of St Bavon at the cost of the wealthy burgess, Joos Vijt, and completed by Jan van Eyck in 1432, six years after his brother's death. The Latin inscription on the frame, contemporary though not written by Jan himself, is unequivocal in its statement to the effect that 'the painter Hubert van Eyck, whom none excels, began the great work which John, second to him in art, completed . . .' What each contributed to this masterpiece is a question that experts have answered differently. As a whole it is a biblical and theological panorama, an imaginative and symbolic conception of an exceptional kind. In this respect it has no parallel in the works known to be by Jan van Eyck alone. It is possible to credit Hubert with a poetic and mystical mind that established the grandeur of plan and to trace the realistic outlook and gifts of Jan in the richness of detail and individual characterization of figures. The combination is effected with a serene and perfect mastery – no work of art could be less appropriately described by the term 'primitive' which it was at one time the custom to apply to the masters of the 15th century.

Of the individual greatness of Jan van Eyck as a realistic observer of contemporary life and as a superb technician, there is no better example than the universally renowned painting in the National Gallery, London, known as 'The Marriage of Giovanni Arnolfini and Giovanna Cenami' (see plate 38). The masterly handling of a double portrait, the perspective and sense of space in the setting, the lustrous brilliance of the oil technique, come first among its attributes, though it is also a fascinating social document, with much to tell of life in Bruges. The portraits are of members of the Italian colony in Bruges, still the international centre of trade. Giovanni Arnolfini was a merchant from Lucca, established in the Flemish city for thirteen years when the picture was painted in 1434 and with many more years still to spend there. Giovanna Cenami, his fiancée, was the daughter of another Lucchese merchant. They are wearing the rich and heavy garments dictated by Burgundian fashion, no doubt of Brugeois manufacture and appropriate to a private marriage ceremony of which the artist, to judge by his signature, 'Johannes de eyck fuit hic' has been an actual witness. Giovanni's hat with its high crown and broad brim is one of those felts made from beaver hair at Bruges, expensive and much in vogue among men cultivating distinction. Giovanna's apple-green dress (van Eyck may have gained from the painters of Cologne the secret of preserving the glow of the colour in paint) falls in the long train also considered proper to occasions of ceremony. The onlooker breathes the authentic atmosphere of the room in a tall-windowed, brick-built Bruges mansion, every detail having been scrupulously set down, from the circular mirror to the intricately wrought candelabrum in which the single lighted candle is a symbol of espousal.

In the same year van Eyck embarked on 'The Madonna of Canon Joris van der Paele' now in the Bruges Museum (see plates 17 & 32). The inscription tells that it was painted to the Canon's order on the occasion of his endowing two chapels in the church of St Donatian (the old cathedral of Bruges, destroyed by the French in 1799). The Madonna enthroned has on the one hand the patron saint, Donatian in episcopal robes, on the other, the donor kneeling in prayer with his own patron saint, St George, beside him in full armour. In this masterpiece there are features that gave a model to later artists; the symmetrical framework of composition; the delight in richness of fabric and curious detail such as the sculptured ornament of the throne with its carvings of Cain and Abel and Samson and the Lion; the concentration on individual human character. The artist's consistent realism turns the saints into living beings, although it is the donor that most holds attention. Heavily jowled, the course of every wrinkle and vein exactly traced, his spectacles poised over the Gothic script of a page in his breviary, Canon George is an unforgettable personality.

One of the greatest portrait painters, van Eyck was a master also of the distant view, such as appears in the 'Madonna of Chancellor Rolin', now in the Louvre,

Fig. 13   Portrait of Margareta van Eyck, by Jan van Eyck, 1439. (12½ × 10in., 31.3 × 25cm.) *Bruges, Groeningemuseum.*

where behind the resolute form of Philip the Good's minister and beyond Roman-esque columns and arches, the Netherlandish city takes on pictorial enchantment and a river (painted perhaps with a memory of the Meuse) winds towards far-off heights. (A similar view occurs in Roger van der Weyden's picture of 'St Luke painting the Virgin' now at the Museum of Fine Arts, Boston, which is reproduced on the front of the jacket).

The style of Jan van Eyck, who died at Bruges in 1441, is reflected in one way or other in the whole course of Netherlandish painting in the 15th century, although in what one may call the symphonic movement of art from city to city and the individual expression of other masters, there are fascinating variations and dis-tinctions to be observed. Van Eyck's great contemporary, Roger van der Weyden is distinct from him in outlook and is creative in a very different way. Van Eyck established a canon of the craft of oil painting, an objective and impassive realism. Van der Weyden, more temperamental and emotional in expression had a capacity for conveying deep feeling in the characters of his religious themes that contrasts with van Eyck's calm. The two dominated the Netherlandish scene in the first half of the 15th century; as van Eyck added lustre to Bruges, so Roger van der Weyden did to Tournai and Brussels.

This great representative of the Walloon South was born at Tournai in about 1399, the city being at that time French. A shadowy figure stands by his side in youth, as that of Hubert van Eyck mysteriously partners his brother. This enigma is the painter Robert Campin of Tournai (died 1444), probably identical with the anonymous author of a group of related works who is known as the 'Master of Flémalle'. Van der Weyden has been identified with the 'Rogelet de la Pasture' who is recorded as one of Campin's pupils at Tournai. Paintings ascribed to Campin show a fondness for homely interior detail often viewed in a curious perspective, as in the celebrated 'Mérode' triptych of the Annunciation now in the Metropolitan Museum, New York, and the 'Virgin and Child before a Fire-Screen' in the National Gallery, London (see plate 21). The artist was fond of that device so often used with delightful effect in Netherlandish painting – the open window with a view beyond. The right wing of the 'Annunciation' (see plate 22) gives an example in the town view seen through the window of Joseph's workshop. The workshop is such as would belong to a carpenter of the painter's time. It was formerly assumed that Joseph was depicted making mouse-traps from the object on his bench and a similar object on the window-sill. But a recent view is that they represent a type of plane used by carpenters of Campin's day. On the sill it would serve as a shop-sign, visible from the street. In comparison with such works those of van der Weyden show a great difference of character. Both artists gave a certain sculptural quality to form, not perhaps unconnected with the fact that Tournai was then the centre of a school of sculptors. But Campin's phlegmatic feminine type and liking for domesticity of setting are clearly distinct from van der Weyden's more profound ability to trace what have been described as 'the movements of the soul'. More dramatic than most of his other works, the paintings of the Virgin, of Saint Veronica holding the handkerchief with the image of Jesus (see plate 23), and of the robber from a lost Crucifixion (see plate 24), now at Frankfurt, have an emotional power and intensity which obviously relate to the work of van der Weyden. It is generally believed, however, that these works belong to the 'Maître de Flémalle'/Robert Campin and show his style at its splendid best.

The resemblance to Gothic sculpture is perhaps more apparent in van der Weyden's painting, as in the great 'Deposition' (Prado, Madrid) which is like a carved wooden altar infused with colour and emotional life, the Gothic effect heightened by the brackets of architectural detail on either side (see plate 28).

Fig. 14 Portrait of Francesco (formerly called Lionello) d'Este by Roger van der Weyden. (11¾ × 8in., 29.5 × 20.3cm.) *New York, Metropolitan Museum of Art, The Michael Friedsam Collection, 1931.*

8 The Belfry, Bruges, from a nineteenth-century lithograph. (8 × 5¾in., 20.3 × 12.4cm.) *London, British Museum.*

9 Hôtel de Ville and Palais de Justice, Bruges.

10 Hôtel de Ville, Ghent.

11 Quai des Marbriers, Bruges.

8

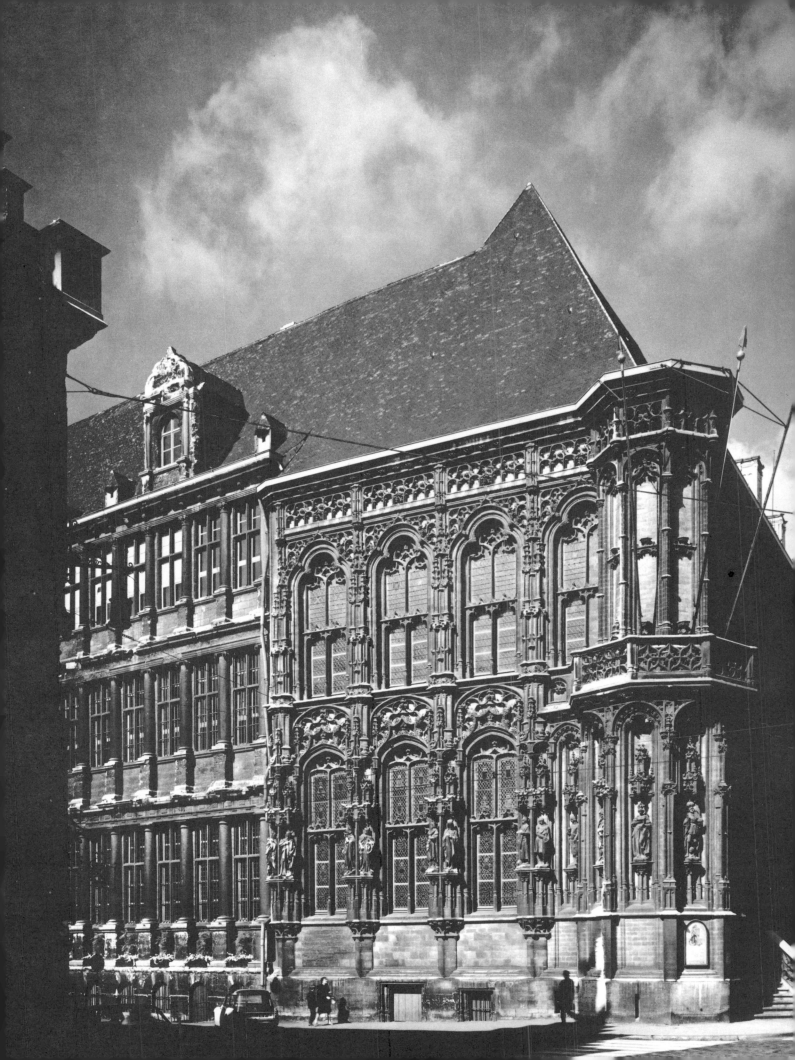

13

14

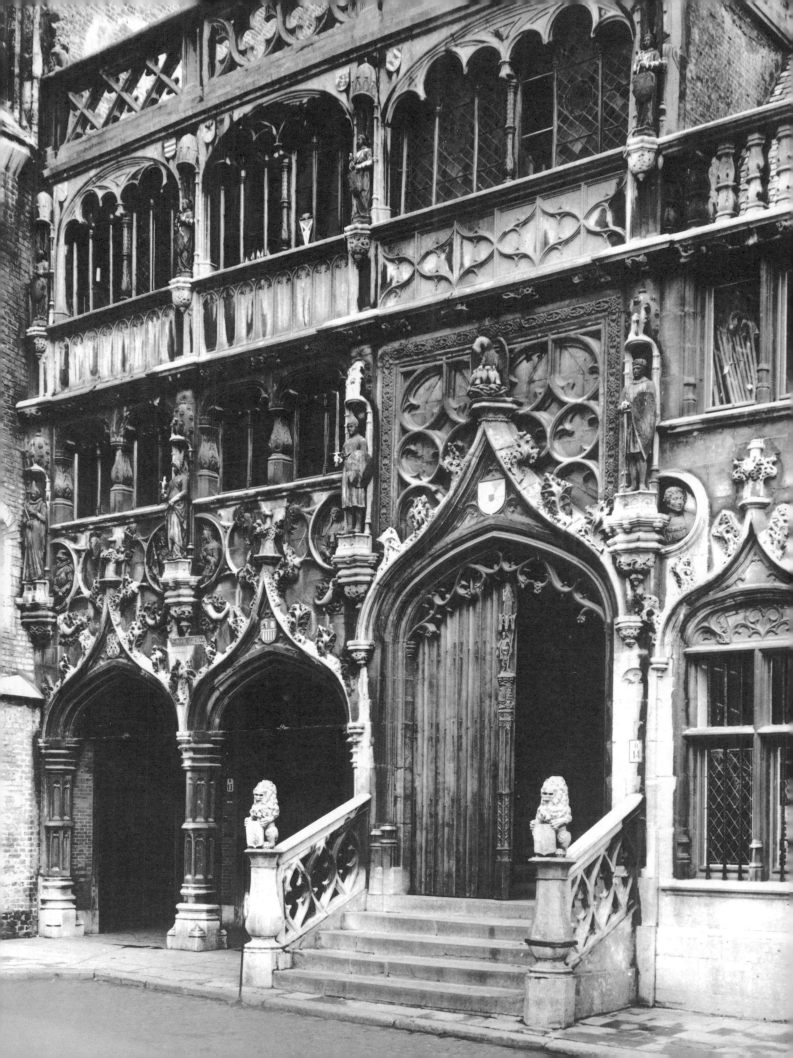

Fig. 15   Bottom right-hand panel showing hell from 'The Last Judgment' by Roger van der Weyden. (Whole polyptych 84 × 216in., 210 × 550cm.) *Beaune, Saint Jean Baptiste et deux Apôtres.*

12   Porte d'Ostende, Bruges.

13   Boucherie (Vleeshal), Antwerp.

14   Façade of the Brewer's House, Antwerp.

15   Flamboyant Gothic front of Chapelle du Saint Sang, Bruges.

Some collaboration has been supposed between master and pupil, in itself possibly indicating their individualities of style. The suggestion has even been put forward (by a present-day art historian, Mojmir S. Frinta in *The Genius of Robert Campin*) that the 'Deposition', assigned to van der Weyden's early maturity, was begun by Campin and finished by his pupil, the former's hand appearing in the weightier and more positive treatment of some figures in contrast with the emotional rendering of grief which only the other could achieve.

This is speculative, however. It is certain that van der Weyden was a master in his own right when in 1436 he came to Brussels – a walled, medieval city very different from the modern Brussels. It is likely that he then changed the French form of his name 'de la Pasture' for the Flemish van der Weyden. At Brussels, where he died in 1464, he was a painter to the municipality. One official commission was a series of paintings on the theme of justice for the Hôtel de Ville (destroyed in 1695). For the guild of painters he pictured St Luke and the Virgin (Museum of Fine Arts, Boston, see front of jacket). The design follows that of Jan van Eyck's 'Chancellor Rolin', the figures being placed on either side of a tiled interior with Romanesque columns opening on a vista of river and town, though the individual grace of style is evident throughout. It is supposed that in St Luke making his silver-point drawing van der Weyden portrayed himself. The type by which he represents the Virgin, with large brow, straight nose, full lower lip and small rounded chin became generally favoured by the Netherlandish painters, just as in Italy painters adapted the ideal type of Filippo Lippi.

In several ways he provided a model for others. In his portraits, more generalized summaries of personality and feature than those of van Eyck – such as the man with an arrow, wearing the Order of the Golden Fleece, identified as Anthony of Burgundy (Brussels), he established a preference for the three-quarter view. He seems also to have initiated the practice of painting the Virgin on one wing of a diptych and on the other the portrait of the donor with hands joined in prayer, as in the case of the 'Philippe de Croy' (Antwerp) and 'Laurent Froimont' (Brussels). His influence in this respect is illustrated by Memlinc's diptych of Martin van Niewenhoven in the Hospital of St John at Bruges (see plate 37).

Through van Eyck and van der Weyden, the two great figures of the first half of the 15th century, the cities of the southern Netherlands became renowned throughout Europe as creative centres. Their personal expeditions abroad and the paintings exported to other countries both deeply impressed painters and connoisseurs. They were 'modern' in the sense of being innovators. Jan van Eyck in Spain and Portugal encouraged the growth of an Iberian school, inspired the genius of the Portuguese master, Nuño Gonçalves. Jean Fouquet in France owed a debt to him, Martin Schongauer among the Germans. The *procédé brugeois* as his method of painting came to be called, assimilated by the Sicilian artist, Antonello da Messina, was taken by the latter to Venice and developed by the Bellinis.

The link of aesthetic sympathy between the cities of Flanders and Italy was strengthened by the visit there of van der Weyden which apparently took place in 1450. He found admiring patrons in Ferrara and Florence to judge by such paintings as the portrait of Francesco (formerly called Lionello) d'Este (Metropolitan Museum, New York, see fig. 14) and the 'Entombment', once in the possession of the Medici family and now in the Uffizi Gallery. In the Netherlands they pointed the way to further brilliant development in a younger generation: Jan van Eyck left no direct studio succession but Petrus Christus who came from Brabant and settled at Bruges, where he died in 1472, continued with a delicate version of his style, the quality of which can be appreciated in his portrait of Edward Grimston of Rishangles, Suffolk (collection of the Earl of Verulam, see plate 79). Painted in

Fig. 16   Detail showing a view of Brussels from the 'Crucifixion' by
Dirck Bouts. (Whole painting 31 × 28⅝in., 88 × 71cm.) *Berlin,
Gemäldegalerie Dhalem, Staatliche Museen.*

1446, it is said to be the earliest portrait of any Englishman abroad.

Van der Weyden's studio at Brussels must have been a busy workshop attracting a number of pupils and assistants. Distinguished among them is Dirck (or Thierry) Bouts who was born at Haarlem between 1415 and 1420 and came southwards like so many Dutch artists after training in his native city. A view of Brussels, appearing in his 'Crucifixion' (Berlin, see fig. 16) marks his stay there. He was steeped in the work of van der Weyden, adopting the facial type of his Madonnas, following him in the practice of introducing details of sculpture that give an illusion of three dimensions. One of van der Weyden's great works was the polyptych of 'The Last Judgment', commissioned by Nicolas Rolin for the Hospice de Beaune which was founded by him in 1442. Its vivid imaginative force and especially its unusual mastery in depicting the nude seem to have inspired Bouts in his 'Fall of the Damned' (Louvre) to give a despairing energy of movement to the nude forms of the condemned (see fig. 15). The journeys of the Netherlandish artists from city to city distributing the fertilizing influence of style are well illustrated in Bouts's career. After Haarlem and Brussels came a stay in Louvain, where he married in 1447. There is then a blank of nearly ten years in his history, in which time it is possible he went back to Holland. This has been suggested by the appearance of mannerisms indicative of van der Weyden's influence in paintings of the Haarlem school. But Bouts returned to Louvain where he died in 1475. At Louvain he painted the 'justice' panels to the commission of the Court of Aldermen, now preserved in the Brussels Museum. His 'The Justice of the Emperor Otho', a history painting done, as was customary, in the dress of his own time, gives a vivid comment on the extravagant richness of 15th-century fashion (see plate 30). The influence of van der Weyden extended to many other painters in Brabant and Flanders. Among them are a number of anonymous minor artists whose work has a con-

42

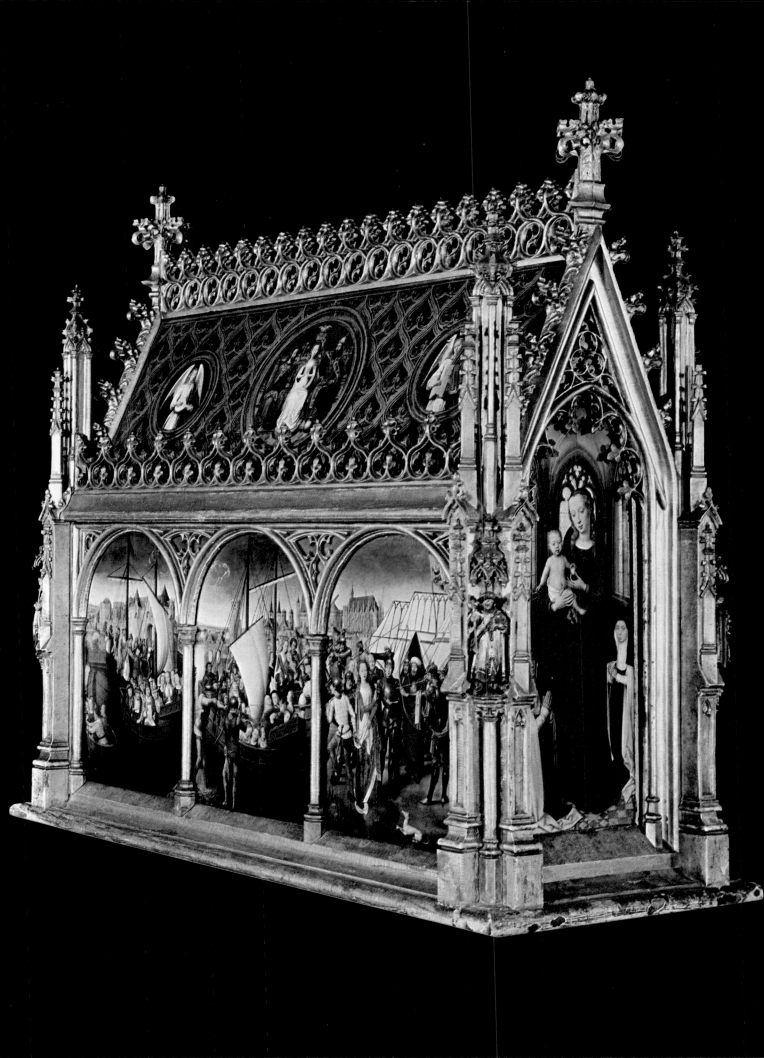

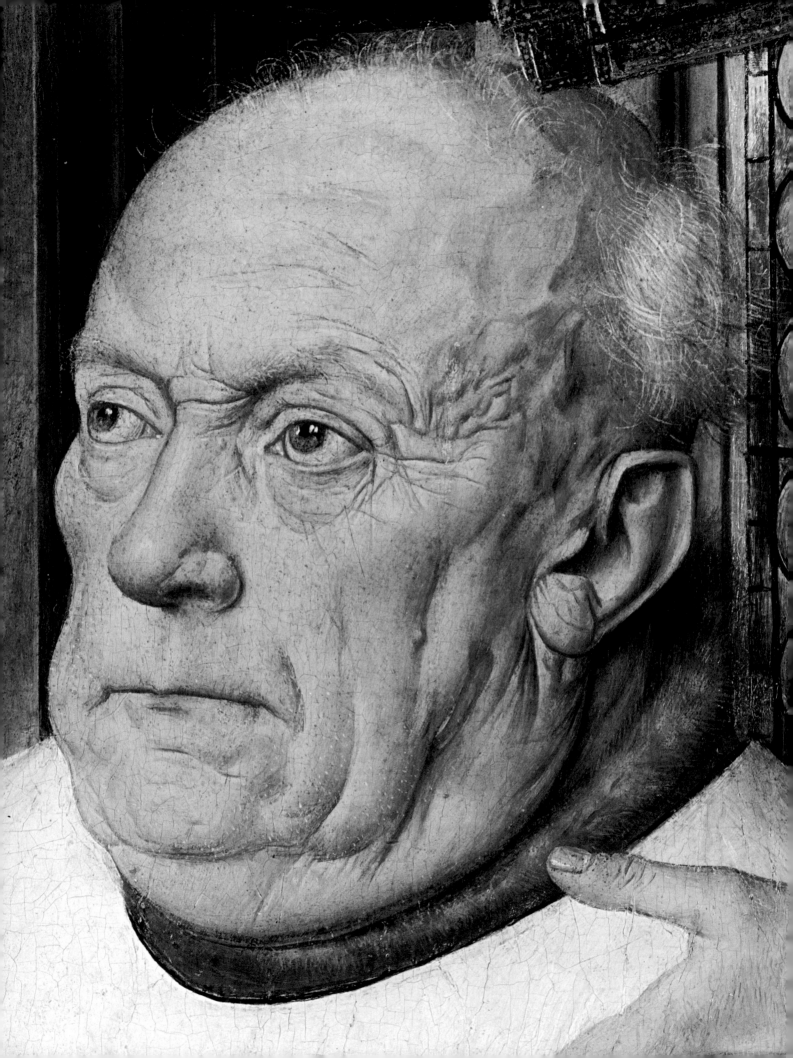

19

20

21

22

23

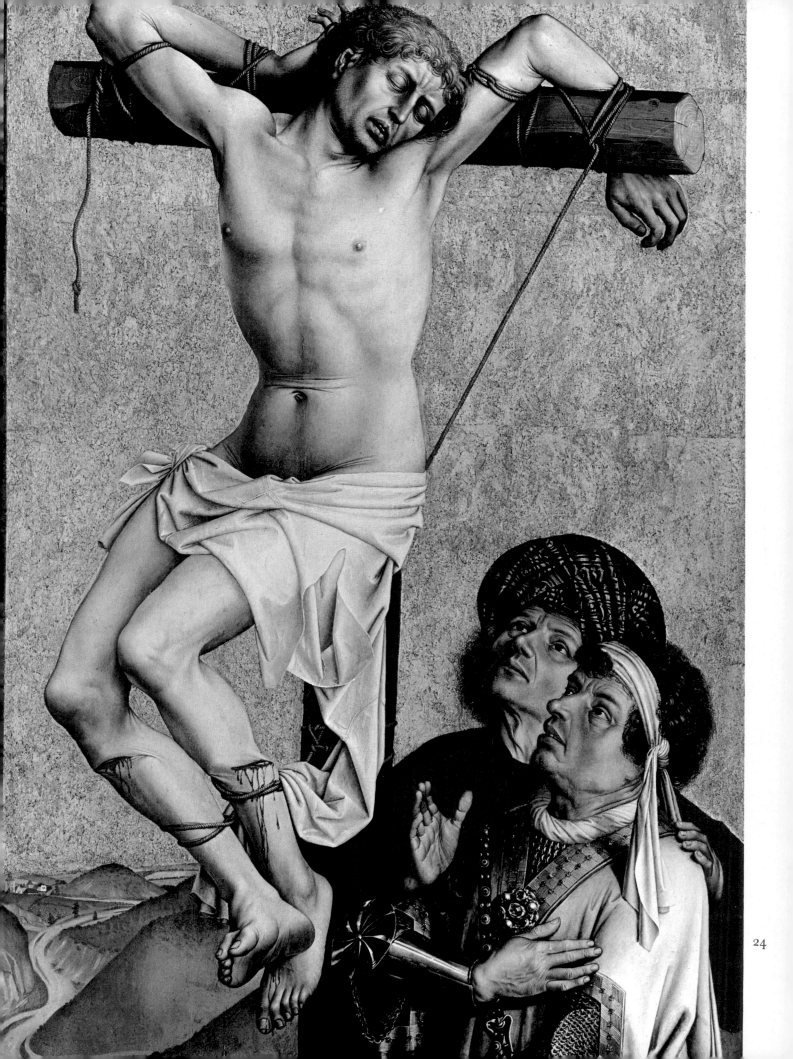

24

Fig. 17 Detail of a harbour
from the 'Virgin and Child' by
the Master of Saint Gudule.
Paris, Louvre.

20 Central panel of 'The
Adoration of the Shepherds'
(Portinari Altarpiece) by
Hugo van der Goes, c. 1475.
(Whole retable 96 × 228in.,
240 × 570cm.) *Florence, Uffizi
Gallery.* (See also plate 60)

21 'Virgin and Child before a
fire-screen' by Robert Campin,
c. 1430. (25 × 19¼in.,
62.5 × 48.4cm.) *London,
National Gallery.*

22 The right wing – Saint
Joseph – from 'The
Annunciation with Donors and
Saint Joseph' (Mérode
triptych) by Robert Campin,
c. 1430. (24 × 10¹⁵⁄₁₆in.,
60 × 27cm.) *New York, The
Metropolitan Museum of Art,
The Cloisters Collection.*

23 Saint Veronica, centre
panel from a retable, by the
Maître de Flémalle, c. 1440.
(59 × 24in., 147.5 × 60cm.)
*Frankfurt, Städelsches
Kunstinstitut.*

24 The Robber, from a part of
a Crucifixion, by the Maître de
Flémalle, c. 1420. (52½ × 36in.,
131.2 × 90cm.) *Frankfurt,
Städelsches Kunstinstitut.*

siderable charm: the 'Master of the Barbara Legend', so called from the triptych of scenes from the life of St Barbara, now distributed between the Brussels Museum and the Chapelle du Saint Sang at Bruges; the Bruges 'Master of the Legend of St Lucy' whose attachment to the city is signalized by the detail showing its belfry in the scenes from the life of the saint, c. 1480 in St Jacques, Bruges (see fig. 4). The 'Master of St Gudule' at Brussels follows van der Weyden's scheme of composition in the 'Virgin and Child' (Diocesan Museum, Liège), adding fascinating contemporary detail in the finery of the figures at the background parapet who look out at the high-pooped ships in the harbour (see fig. 17).

Ghent and Bruges are prominent in the renewed brilliance of Netherlandish painting in the second half of the 15th century. Hugo van der Goes, born probably about 1440, a master in the Ghent guild in 1467, carries van der Weyden's spiritual and emotional feeling to a new pitch of fervour. No painter is more closely associated with Bruges than Hans Memlinc who brings the threads of Netherlandish art together in placid harmony. There is a haunting resemblance to the life and art of Vincent van Gogh in the troubled mental history of van der Goes and the vehemence of his style. He worked at Ghent until about 1475, being much employed on the decorations accompanying Burgundian festival and ceremony. Then he became a lay-brother in the Augustinian monastery of Roode Kloster (or Rouge Cloître) some miles south of Brussels in the Forest of Soignies, and died there in 1482. He had continued to paint at the monastery and to move about freely, going in 1478 to make a valuation of paintings by Bouts at Louvain, where he was hailed as a famous master. It was on his return from a visit to Cologne in 1481 that he fell victim to a mania from which he did not recover.

The painting that gives the key to his art is the great 'Adoration of the Shepherds' (Uffizi Gallery, Florence), commonly known as the 'Portinari Altarpiece' (see plates 20 & 60). Like the van Eyck 'Arnolfini' a sign of the intercourse between Flanders and Italy, it was painted for the agent of the Medici at Bruges, Tommaso Portinari, who appears in it as donor with his wife and children. The majestic calm of the Virgin contrasts with the surrounding agitation of the composition, the flutter of angels, the varied expressions of awe and astonishment in the shepherds. He seems to impart something of his own psychological intensity to their rough features. A similar contrast of tranquillity and restless movement and expression is to be found in the 'Death of the Virgin' (Bruges Museum) (see plate 77). The emotional mood conveyed by colour and gesture, the psychological force of his painting made a great impression on his contemporaries, on the miniaturists of Ghent and Bruges towards the end of the century, on Ghirlandaio, and on other Italian painters who were able to study the Portinari altarpiece. His realism in the portrayal of character was imparted to the 'Master of Moulins' (identified with the French painter, Jean Perréal). His key of emotional colour links him with the great Grünewald in Germany. As a draughtsman also his talent was outstanding as the enchanting drawing of 'Rachel and Jacob', attributed to him and now at Christ Church, Oxford, shows; one of the few remaining drawings from this period of Flemish art, it has an unusually idyllic and lyrical quality (see fig. 18).

Hans Memlinc, the most idyllic of the Netherlandish masters, was German in origin, born somewhere between 1430 and 1440 at Seligenstadt near Frankfurt. He must have been about thirty when he came to Bruges, by which time it is likely he had had a good deal of experience in the Rhineland and perhaps at Brussels. Less forceful than van Eyck, more mundane than van der Weyden, he added a singular personal refinement to the Netherlandish style which his great predecessors had formed. Settled at Bruges he delighted the foreign visitors, diplomatic and mercantile, and the town magistrates, like Niewenhoven, with his altarpieces and

51

portraits. A reminder of the intercourse between Flanders and England is the 'Donne' triptych, which eventually came through a long family succession into the collection of the Dukes of Devonshire, from which it was acquired by the National Gallery, London, in 1957 (see plate 34). The triptych was painted for Sir John Donne, knighted by Edward IV in 1471. The King himself had then not long returned from his refuge at Bruges where he was entertained by Louis de Gruuthuse (and seems to have acquired his host's taste for the illuminated manuscript). The scales in the long-drawn Wars of the Roses tipped at last in his favour. It was after his decisive victory for the House of York over the Lancastrian forces at the battle of Tewkesbury that he knighted Donne who subsequently enjoyed royal favour. The triptych was probably painted when Sir John was on a diplomatic mission to Flanders in 1477. A lean and careworn-looking diplomat he kneels on the left, Lady Donne on the right, both wearing the Yorkist collar of roses and suns. The small figure peering from behind a column on the left outer wing of the painting has been supposed the artist himself, indulging perhaps a quiet humour in assigning himself this unobtrusive place (see fig. 19).

Memlinc executed a number of paintings also for the ancient foundation at Bruges, the Hospital of St John, where many products of his genius still remain, among them the famous St Ursula Shrine (see plate 16). A fanciful legend (of the 17th century) represents him as arriving at Bruges, a wounded soldier, being cared for at the Hospital and in gratitude making it pictorial gifts. In fact, the various donors of such works as 'The Adoration of the Magi' and the 'Pietà' are named. A masterpiece at the Hospital is 'The Mystic Marriage of St Catherine', its composition bringing to a delicate perfection the style of the Donne triptych (see plate 31). It has been supposed that Memlinc's wife, Anne de Valkenaere, brought him a handsome dowry but his wealth was no doubt due to his own efforts. Few citizens of Bruges paid more in taxes. With his wife and three children he lived in one of the large stone mansions that were the evidence of fortune. He died at Bruges in 1495, mourned as 'the most excellent painter of all the Christian world'.

There were still brilliant painters to come at Bruges, continuing the tradition established by Memlinc into the early 16th century, though they should be seen in relation to the political and economic changes, later to be considered. Meanwhile, another splendour of the Burgundian era must be chronicled, the glorious supplement to painting that is to be found in Netherlandish tapestry. As textiles had so vital a part in the growth and prosperity of the cities it was only to be expected that the production of tapestries should become a highly-developed industry. Richly figured after the design of some master painter and as rich in substance as in design, with their multitudinous threads of gold and silver, silk and fine wool, they had a sumptuousness that appealed as strongly to the Burgundian connoisseurs as the illuminated manuscript. They were not only the pleasure of the Dukes in their own châteaux. Often they were diplomatic gifts, such as the tapestries which Philip the Good commissioned for presentation to the Pope. Foreign rulers and princes were eager to possess them. Perhaps the result of a royal commission from England, the great 'Devonshire Hunting Tapestries', now preserved in the Victoria and Albert Museum (see plate 67) were woven on the looms of Tournai between 1425 and 1430. They seem to be related to the occasion of Henry VI's marriage to Margaret, daughter of King René of Anjou, and in some way became the property of the ancestors of the Dukes of Devonshire in the pre-Tudor age.

Several Flemish cities had their flourishing period of tapestry production. Arras, for example, was a great centre from the 14th to the 15th century; some of the weavers and many of the products came to England, where the word 'arras' came to do duty for any woven wall-hanging, as in *Hamlet* the concealment of

Fig. 18 Detail from the meeting of Rachel and Jacob, drawing by van der Goes. (15 × 21½in., 37.5 × 53.9cm.) *Oxford, Christ Church*.

Fig. 19 Detail from the left panel of the 'Donne' triptych, with a supposed self-portrait of Hans Memlinc. *London, National Gallery*.

Polonius 'behind the arras' is a reminder. The *Galleria degli Arazzi* of the Vatican gives the Italian equivalent of 'arras' for tapestry in general. The patronage of Charles the Bold supported the craft at Arras though it declined there after the death of the ambitious and warlike Duke in 1477. Tournai was a rival centre. A famous set of tapestries depicting the Trojan War was woven in 1472 by Pasquier Grenier of Tournai to the order of the magistrates of Bruges for presentation to Charles the Bold.

Brussels where the guild of *tapissiers* was formed about 1448 acquired its greatest prestige in the 16th century. Its reputation for tapestry was international. The 'History of Abraham' preserved at Hampton Court marks the interest of Henry VIII of England. Like the painters, the master weavers were invited to work abroad. Just as the friend of van der Goes at Ghent, Joos van Wassenhove, went to Urbino to paint for the great Renaissance patron, Federigo da Montefeltro, so weavers from Brussels formed a colony of craft at Mantua in the second half of the 15th century. As van Wassenhove, known in Italy as 'Giusto di Guanda' became the associate of Piero della Francesca, so the Brussels craftsmen came into the sphere of Andrea Mantegna who supplied them with designs.

The development of tapestry was closely parallel to that of painting. The weaver was required by guild rules to work from designs supplied by painters, except for some latitude of original effort in the production of *verdures*, tapestries confined to decorative leaf and flower patterns. The late-Gothic preoccupations of the painter, the scenes of hunting and falconry, the knights and ladies in their ornate apparel, the flowers, minutely naturalistic, that made almost a herbal of many an altarpiece, took on new values on the often vast tapestry scale. Besides such subjects as 'The Deposition' exemplified by a magnificent Brussels tapestry of the early 16th century (see plate 36), preserved in the great collection of the Palais du Cinquantenaire at Brussels, the chivalrous and legendary themes of the manuscript book were given enlargement. The war of Troy becomes a medieval siege, the ancient Greeks wear elaborate coats of mail and the city of Priam and Helen acquires the turrets and battlemented walls of the Netherlands.

Tapestry production at Brussels outlasted the Burgundian era. The municipal stamp which it was made compulsory to affix – a red shield supported by two Bs – was still a hallmark of superlative quality in the 16th century. But changes were then taking place with momentous effects on all the arts. They were part of the general change in which politics, religious ideas, economic circumstances and altering attitudes to art contributed to a new pattern of life. The conflicts and strivings of the past paled before the intensities of this upheaval.

Fig. 20   Detail from the 'History of Abraham' tapestries, depicting the purchase of the field of Ephron. *Hampton Court Palace. Copyright reserved.*

Fig. 21   Detail from the 'History of Abraham' tapestries, showing the return of Sara by the Egyptians. *Hampton Court Palace. Copyright reserved.*

The factors that made for change were many. Economic circumstances affected the relative importance of the cities. The end of Burgundian rule and the advent of the oppressive House of Habsburg brought a long train of calamity. The great split of ideas and beliefs that came with the Reformation and the efforts to counter it by Church and State were drastic in result. The arts were influenced in a variety of ways, by religion and politics and by the commanding position Italy occupied at the height of the Renaissance, causing artists to look to Rome both for training and modes of expression which undermined the old self-contained character of Netherlandish art.

Economic change is dramatically seen in the decline of Bruges and the rise of Antwerp. In the 15th century Bruges became entirely cut off from the sea. The Zwijn, too much banked against flood and steadily silting up over a long period, had been inexorably reducing the sea-going trade. By about 1480 no large ship could reach the seaward outpost of Damme. When the architect, engineer and sculptor Lancelot Blondeel proposed the construction of a new port and ship canal in 1546 it was too late. Antwerp had gained the monopoly of the North Sea traffic. Nor was Bruges, by then impoverished and suffering from various distresses, in a position to undertake any such ambitious scheme. There were other reasons for decline. The medieval economic system had irksome restrictions which inclined merchants and foreign traders to seek fresh ground and to use more flexible methods of dealing with banking, capital and credit. By 1560 the commercial embassies of other countries were established at Antwerp instead of Bruges while as many as five hundred ships entered or left Antwerp's busy port every day.

The rights and liberties of the Flemish communes were whittled away during the rule of Charles the Bold from 1467 to 1476. They were compelled to pay out large sums to support his thirst for conquest and war against France. After his death at the battle of Nancy they hoped for better things from his young and popular daughter, Marie of Burgundy, only to find themselves saddled with a new and worse tyrant in the Archduke Maximilian, the son of the Emperor Frederick III, who was married to Marie in 1477. An ambitious, treacherous and irresponsible youth, he dragged on the war, plundered the burghers afresh, pawned the Burgundian plate and treasure to the house of Medici and sold a large part of the great ducal library. On the death of Marie in 1482, the succession of her little son, Philip, and the legal position of Maximilian became acute questions which brought the burghers of Ghent and Bruges into direct conflict with their rulers. The prolonged struggle that followed, with all its intricacies of plotting and ferocities of bloodshed, involving the period of Maximilian's imprisonment in the Cranenburg at Bruges and the execution of the magistrates supposedly in his pay, ended at last in Maximilian's victory. Bruges, defeated and starving, bereft of trade, pillaged by mercenaries, was in 1490 also compelled to pay a huge indemnity.

The surprising thing is that in spite of all this civic tumult and misfortune artists continued to work for some time yet at Bruges with apparent placidity in a final phase of the established Netherlandish style. The city gained a distinguished

25   The Month of January: The Duc de Berry seated at table, from *Les Très Riches Heures* by Pol, Jeannequin and Herman de Limbourg, c. 1411. (6¾ × 6in., 17 × 15.3cm.) *Chantilly, Musée Condé.*

26   Leaf from the Ghent School Book of Hours. (6½ × 4½in., 16.5 × 11.5cm.) *Bruges, Abbaye de Saint André.*

27   Crucifixion from the *Pontifical de l'Eglise de Sens* by Simon Marmion. (14⅛ × 9½in., 35.3 × 24.2cm.) *Brussels, Bibliothèque Royale* Ms. 9215 fo. 129.

28   'The Deposition' by Roger van der Weyden, c. 1460. (78¾ × 104in., 200 × 263cm.) *Madrid, Museo del Prado.*

successor to Memlinc in Gerard David, born about 1460 at Oudewater near Utrecht. He may have been trained at Haarlem where Albert van Oudewater, his pupil Geertgen tot St Jans and Dirck Bouts were noted for their landscape backgrounds, a feature in which David excelled. He was admitted to the Bruges guild of painters in 1484 and attained some eminence in civic life. He was made dean of the Guild of St Luke in 1501 and in the same year married Cornelia, artist-daughter of Jacob Cnoop, dean of the Goldsmiths' guild. In 1508 he became a member of the exclusive *Société de Notre-Dame à l'Arbre Sec*, a body responsible for the maintenance of a chapel between Damme and Sluys. In 1521 he was rich enough to make a substantial loan to the Carmelite Convent of Sion. It was repaid in 1523 when he was ill and shortly before his death. A document places his tomb under the tower of Notre-Dame, Bruges.

David was in the city at the time when Maximilian was held captive in the Cranenburg on the Grand'Place. In the course of W. H. James Weale's researches into the Bruges Archives from 1860 onwards he found that David was employed to paint over the iron bars on the windows so that Maximilian should be the less conscious of being confined. The burghers still hoped for compromise.

The events that followed, the trial, torture and execution of the burgomaster, judge and aldermen accused of corrupt activity on Maximilian's behalf have symbolic reference in the two paintings (now in the Bruges Museum) from the series carried out by David between 1487 and 1498 for the court room in the Hôtel de Ville (see plate 72). Illustrating Herodotus's story of Sisamnes, corrupt judge of ancient Egypt, convicted and ordered to be flayed by King Cambyses, the artist depicts the gruesome operation unflinchingly and even phlegmatically.

Apart from this indirect comment on the tumult of contemporary events he is as quietly affectionate in detail as Memlinc before him. His love for Bruges is apparent in the minute labour he lavishes on glimpses of its architecture, the background of the trial in which the church of St Jacques can be identified, the Gothic porch in the flaying scene with the coats of arms of the Counts of Flanders and the city of Bruges. The Hôtel de Ville appears in the background of 'The Marriage at Cana' (Louvre), the tower of Notre-Dame, Bruges, in the wing of a diptych showing an ecclesiastic praying (National Gallery, London). His skill as a landscape artist is shown in the detail from the 'Baptism of Christ' (Groeningemuseum, Bruges, see plates 59 & 74). In spite of Bruges's troubles it was still an art market in the first half of the 16th century, with a considerable export of paintings to other countries. It still attracted painters from elsewhere, like the pupils of David, Adriaen Ysenbrandt who lived at Bruges until 1551 and Ambrosius Benson (originally perhaps Benzoni), a native of Lombardy who died at Bruges in 1550. Illuminated manuscripts produced in quantity for export gave employment to numbers of bookbinders, calligraphers, and miniature painters. Both David and his wife Cornelia practised miniature painting. The fame of Simon Benning, long eminent in the Bruges guild, spread to Italy and seven years after his death at Bruges in 1561 he was mentioned by Vasari as 'the most agreeable colourist among the Flemings'.

The end of the late-medieval phase of Flemish or Netherlandish art is signalized by David and his followers. Artists were now moving to Antwerp in the wake of wealth and Antwerp was not only the centre of a new capitalism but of Renaissance ideas and the Humanist culture that was their expression. The city had only had a minor share in the great expansion of medieval trade, though a branch of the Hansa was established there in the 14th century. The plan of the magnificent cathedral church of Notre-Dame, the largest in the Netherlands, bears witness to the ambitious conceptions of the 14th and 15th centuries. The graceful north tower that rises

Fig. 22   An ecclesiastic praying, right wing of a diptych by Gerard David. (13⅜ × 10½in., 33.5 × 26.3cm.) *London, National Gallery.*

29   Detail of Saint Mary Magdalene, right wing of the 'Braque' triptych by Roger van der Weyden. (16¼ × 13½in., 41 × 34.5cm.) *Paris, Musée du Louvre.*

30   Panel from 'The Justice of the Emperor Otho' by Dirck Bouts, 1464. (123 × 72in., 307.5 × 180cm.) *Brussels, Musées Royaux des Beaux Arts de Belgique.*

31   'The Mystic Marriage of Saint Catherine' by Hans Memlinc, 1479. (Centre panel 70 × 70in., 174 × 174cm.) *Bruges, Hôpital Saint Jean.*

so superbly above the Scheldt and the spreading plain, completed by Dominicus de Waghemakere in the 16th century was still in the late-Gothic style (see plate 6 & fig. 2). There was still a medieval spirit in the processions of merchants to their places of business, preceded by musicians playing on fife and viol. But the evidences of modernity were noticeable. The belfry, a feature which had lost its original function but elsewhere remained a symbol of communal pride, was destroyed as a useless anachronism. The symbol of new enterprise and function was the Bourse (see fig. 23)

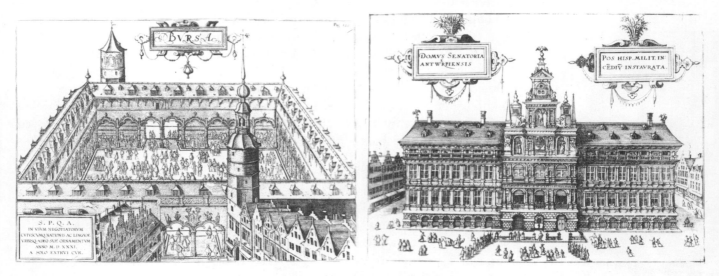

Fig. 23 *Left* The Bourse, Antwerp. *Right* Hôtel de Ville, Antwerp.
Both from Guicciardini, published by Plantin 1581. *Antwerp, Museum Plantin-Moretus.*

32 'The Madonna of Canon Joris van der Paele' by van Eyck, 1434. (48 × 62in., 120 × 155cm.) *Bruges, Groeningemuseum.* (See also plate 17)

33 The whole polyptych open – 'The Adoration of the Lamb' by van Eyck. (146 × 195in., 365 × 487cm.) *Ghent, Cathedral of Saint Bavon.* (See also plates 18 & 19)

34 Centre panel of the 'Donne' triptych by Hans Memlinc, c. 1470. (27 × 28in., 67.5 × 70cm.) *London, National Gallery.*

35 Centre panel – 'The Eucharist' – from 'The Triptych of the Seven Sacraments' by Roger van der Weyden, c. 1445. (78½ × 38in., 200 × 97cm.) *Antwerp, Musée Royal des Beaux Arts.*

36 'The Deposition', early sixteenth-century tapestry. *Brussels, Palais du Cinquantenaire.*

built in 1531 at the enormous cost of 300,000 crowns – so impressive to the English 'King's merchant', Sir Thomas Gresham, that after the disturbances of the century caused him to leave the Netherlands in 1567 he built his Exchange in London on a similar plan. The tall and picturesque guild houses of the Grand'Place mark the transition from Gothic to Renaissance in architectural style. Their ornateness is in contrast with the classical severity of the Hôtel de Ville (1561), the first to be built in the Netherlands in an Italianate style (see fig. 23), the architect Cornelis de Vriendt taking the Florentine palace as his model.

Transition in pictorial art is vividly exemplified by the work of Quinten Metsys (or Massys) (1466–1530). The son of a smith who was also clockmaker and architect to the city of Louvain where he was born, it was there also that he became apprenticed as a painter, probably in the studio of Dirck Bouts. Through him he absorbed the influence of Memlinc and van der Weyden which appears in his earlier work. One of the first artist migrants to Antwerp, he settled there in 1491 and continued to paint for some time in the spirit of Memlinc and with the traditional minuteness of finish. In the atmosphere of Antwerp and possibly through a visit to Italy, which was now becoming part of an artist's education, his outlook changed, and he developed into an artist of a new type, moving in scholarly circles, the friend of the great Humanists, Erasmus and Sir Thomas More. Erasmus commissioned him to paint his portrait as a gift to More. The humanist expression of countenance, at once learned and kindly, appears also in his portrait of the secretary to the city of Antwerp, Peter Gillis, or as the classical fashion of the time translated his name, Petrus Aegidius (Longford Castle, see plate 81). He is depicted with an appropriate background of learned books, his finger resting on one of Erasmus's works.

Metsys was important and prosperous at Antwerp. His house with its external frescoes was a show-piece pointed out for the admiration of visitors, among them

32

33

34

35

36

37

38

39

Prologue de lacteur.

Les fais des anciens doit
on voulentiers lire ouyr
et diligentement retenir
car ilz peuent valoir et
donner bon exemple aux hardis en arme

40

the great Albrecht Dürer on his journey through the Netherlands. He painted religious subjects in which both Flemish and Italian elements of style appear, like 'The Entombment' (Antwerp Museum) his masterpiece of 1511, commissioned by the carpenters' guild for the altar of the cathedral. The example of Leonardo seems to have been before him in his painting of the Madonna. But he shows also how in the worldly city of his time the devotional theme was being supplemented by the secular. The subject of the banker or money lender and his wife (see plate 58), weighing their gold and making up their accounts may have had some moral point but could be taken merely to reflect the preoccupations of a city of bankers. That the detail of ledgers, coins and scales and the absorption of the couple in their calculation were fascinating to the artist's clients may be gathered from the popularity of the *genre*. Metsys's own several versions were imitated by his sons, Cornelis and Jan, and in a more satirical vein as a criticism of usury by Marinus van Reymerswael (*c.* 1497–1570) (see fig. 24).

The secular trend appears also in the scenes of popular life which were later to become so characteristic of both Dutch and Flemish art; and in the growing importance attached to landscape. Pieter Aertsen, Dutch in origin, born at Amsterdam *c.* 1508, who settled at Antwerp where he died in 1575, painted kitchen and market scenes (see fig. 25) and an early example of the intimate kitchen *genre* is 'The Maidservant' (watching a fowl roasting on a spit) in the Brussels Museum.

An affection for landscape had always been characteristic of Netherlandish art, sometimes as a background view of flat plain and winding river, sometimes as in the backgrounds of Gerard David suggesting the rocky banks of the Meuse and the more luxuriant scenery of the region. Landscape was developed further by Metsys, and it became for the first time the principal feature of interest in what were ostensibly biblical subjects in the work of his friend, Joachim Patinir. Patinir, who was born probably at Dinant towards the end of the 15th century and settled in

Fig. 24 'The Tax Collectors' by Marinus van Reymerswael. (26 × 20½ in., 65 × 51.6cm.) *Antwerp, Musée Royal des Beaux Arts.*

37 Diptych of Martin van Niewenhoven, by Hans Memlinc, 1487. *Left,* a portrait of van Niewenhoven. (Each 16½ × 13in., 41.3 × 32.5cm.) *Bruges, Hôpital Saint Jean.*

38 'The Marriage of Giovanni Arnolfini and Giovanna Cenami' by Jan van Eyck, 1434. (32¼ × 23½in., 81.8 × 60cm.) *London, National Gallery.*

39 'A woman', ascribed to Robert Campin, before 1430. (16 × 11in., 40.7 × 27.9cm.) *London, National Gallery.*

40 Grisaille representation of a Flemish town and its gateway from the *Chroniques de Charlemagne,* by Jean Le Tavernier, 1460. (Size of miniature 7⅞ × 6⅝in., 20 × 16.5cm.) *Brussels, Bibliothèque Royale* Ms. 9066 fo. 11.

Fig. 25 'Peasants at Market' by Pieter Aertsen. (45 × 63in., 112.8 × 157.5cm.) *Antwerp, Musée Royal des Beaux Arts.*

73

Antwerp where he died in 1524, specialized in a type of river and mountainous scenery even more suggestive of the Ardennes and the Meuse than the work of David (see plates 75 & 76).

Transition in terms of style is to be seen in the mannerisms resulting from an acquaintance with Italy and the art of the Renaissance masters. Painters in every part of the Netherlands felt the Italian influence – Jan Mostaert from Haarlem (c. 1475–1555), Jan Gossaert from Maubeuge (c. 1480–c. 1536), Bernard van Orley of Brussels (1488–1541), Lambert Lombard of Liège (c. 1506–1566) are notable among the numerous artists known as 'Romanists'. The great series of cartoons from New Testament history by Raphael, entrusted to the weavers of Brussels for carrying out in tapestry, must have made a strong impression on artists in Brussels. This influence appears in the altarpieces of van Orley, such as 'The Trials of Job' in the Brussels Museum as well as in his designs for tapestry (see plates 92 & 93) and stained glass, of which the grandiose windows of the Chapel of the Sacrament in St Gudule Cathedral provide an example (see fig. 26). In all the arts and crafts the contact between the Netherlands and Italy was now apparent. The architect and sculptor, Cornelis Floris (1518–1575) and the sculptor Jan Vredeman de Vries developed Italian forms of sculptural ornament that came to be known as the 'Floris style' and were much imitated in Germany. A Cambrai sculptor, Jean Boulogne (1529–1608) settled in Florence, to become illustrious and Italianized in name as Giovanni Bologna, and though he never returned to the Netherlands many young Netherlandish artists sought him out and imitated his style. In the form of decorative craft that is so much associated with Belgium, the production of bobbin and needlepoint lace, it seems likely that from about the beginning of the 16th century Flanders followed Italian example, using the same pattern books as the Venetian lacemakers.

Yet the changes so far considered have been to a large extent a shifting pattern of aesthetic influences. Forces of another kind affecting the whole of Europe bore down on the Netherlands with a particular intensity. The 16th century was the time when the great cleft in religion opened to become wide and irreparable, when the printed book became not only the instrument of humanist learning but a theological weapon, when the 'Holy Roman' Empire, attaining a fantastic enlargement under Charles V, imposed the combined weight of religious intolerance and political tyranny. The cities of the Netherlands had never been tolerant of outside authority though their various insurrections had commonly been against financial extortion. Their first great age of art, however, displays no unrest of thought, no hint of social criticism or satire. Painters, though allowed to introduce much mundane detail into their works of religious character, give no suggestion other than that of a calm and dutiful piety. The critical spirit first becomes evident in the literary products of Humanism. Printed biblical texts encouraged independent study and inquiry. They established even an independence of language. Thus the Low Frankish dialect became distinct as Dutch in an Old Testament published at Delft in 1477. Satire of a misgoverned world appears in the rhyming couplets of *The Ship of Fools* by the German poet, Sebastian Brant; it had a wide circulation and no doubt inspired Erasmus's *In Praise of Folly* (1509) which in playful earnest mocked both kings and churchmen. It heralded the pamphlets of Luther against the abuses of the Church and his open split with the papacy in 1517. It was not long before his doctrines were being preached in the northern Netherlands and thence spread to the south.

In the period of humanist satire there appears a Netherlandish artist very different from any that had gone before and, in fantastic invention, one of the most remarkable artists the world has known, Jeronimus Anthonissen van Aken, now usually referred to as Jerome, or Hieronymus, Bosch. He was born at the provincial

Fig. 26   Detail of stained glass, designed by Bernard van Orley. *Brussels, Chapel of Saint Sacrement de Miracle, Church of Saint Gudule.*

41   Boss of wooden ceiling of the Grande Salle in the Hôtel de Ville, Bruges.

42   The tower of the Church of Saint Gudule, Brussels.

43   Exterior view of the apsidal chapels of Notre-Dame au Sablon, Brussels.

44   The main portal and turrets of the church of Saint Nicolas, Ghent.

town of north Brabant, 's-Hertogenbosch (or Bois-le-Duc) probably about 1450, the son of a painter, Anthonissen van Aken. He seems to have lived and worked only in his native town until his death in 1516. Little is known of him personally. He married and inherited a property near the village of Oirschot from his brother-in-law in 1484, was a leading member of the lay Brotherhood of Our Lady for which his father had painted altarpieces, acted in religious plays and sang in the church choir. 's-Hertogenbosch had industries that made it prosperous, a prosperity helping to account for its great church of St John, new in his time, for which he painted altarpieces and designed stained-glass windows. But he was not unknown in his own day. He had noble patrons and at a later date became, surprisingly, a favourite painter of Philip II of Spain, who collected some of his best works in Madrid.

The origin and intention of his art are still the subject of much speculation. He seems full of strange enigmas, ambiguous in relation to the age in which he lived. In his invention of demons and paintings of hell he may be thought to hark back to the decaying superstitions of the Middle Ages, to uncover an aspect of the Netherlandish mind which the realistic painters who preceded him had not revealed; the belief in sorcery, the sense of the sataric and grotesque expressed in the gargoyle and the monsters of the illuminated border, the love of performances in which the farcical and the fiendish were united, the mysticism of the symbol that gave a variety of secondary meanings to natural objects. Yet the exotic plants and animals he painted in his Eden suggest his interest in the new worlds of contemporary exploration.

Fig. 27   Detail from the central panel of 'The Garden of Terrestrial Delights' by Hieronymus Bosch. *Madrid, Museo del Prado.*

From another point of view Bosch is subtle, psychological, even Freudian, in the creation of a dream world that contains much of sex. His is not the crudely imagined medieval hell; in the great triptych in the Prado known as 'The Garden of Terrestrial Delights' from its central panel, his men and women seem to pass through the conflagrations of sin into a grey, still underworld where they might be imagined as the helpless victims of their own desires (see plates 63 & 66 & fig. 27).

The significance of his work is still variously interpreted. So little does he conform to the conventional treatment of the religious subject that it has been ingeniously argued that he belonged to an heretical Adamite sect, though this is not more than a theory. But he was certainly unorthodox to an extent that made churchmen suspect heresy. It is not unreasonable – it is even impossible – not to see satire in his art. His painted 'Ship of Fools' is near in date to Brant's literary treatment of the theme. A tonsured priest is one of the undignified company in the boat. His 'The Hay Wain' in the Prado depicts kings and clerics alike in the crowd that pursues the false lure of material satisfaction. Deriving from medieval sources his art seems to convey the disquiet of change and perhaps an intuition of disturbed times to come (see plates 62 & 73).

The doctrines of the Reformers, of Luther first and after him Calvin, spread throughout the Netherlands in the first half of the 16th century. Just as the cities, North and South, had equally contributed to painting so now they shared a growing Protestantism. But they were subject to an authority more powerful and ruthless than any they had yet known. A succession of marriages gave the House of Habsburg world dominion. The Archduke Maximilian who became Emperor in 1493 had an eye to Italian acquisition in marrying Bianca Sforza after the death of Mary of Burgundy. He had eventually to part with Milan and Verona but his son Philip the Fair, by his marriage to Joanna ('the Mad'), daughter of Ferdinand and Isabella, claimed succession to the throne of Spain and all the Spanish possessions. Philip the Fair died in 1506. Ferdinand who, after the death of Isabella, assumed the title of Regent of Castile, because of his daughter's insanity, died in 1516. The son of

Philip and Joanna, Charles, born at Ghent in 1500 went to Spain as joint ruler with his mother when he was seventeen. He was crowned Emperor as Charles V in 1520. He had thus automatically gained a colossal inheritance comprising the imperial Germanic lands, the Netherlands, Burgundy, Spain, Naples and Sicily, and the Spanish possessions in the New World. His authority stretched from Austria through Antwerp to Peru.

It is significant that one of Charles V's first acts was to condemn the subversive

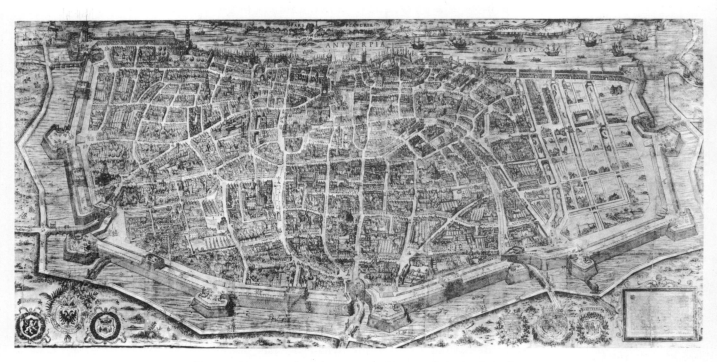

Fig. 28   Bird's eye view of Antwerp by Virgilius Boloniensis (1565).

49   Detail of a gable; Guildhouse on the Quai aux Herbes, Ghent.

50   Interior of the Church of Notre-Dame, Bruges, showing Michelangelo's Madonna and Child in its setting.

51   Detail showing the sculpture on the walled-up gateway of the Hôpital Saint Jean, Bruges.

52   Detail from the Altar of Saint George by Jan Borman the Elder. *Brussels, Musées Royaux d'Art et d'Histoire.*

53   Bronze monument to Duchess Mary of Burgundy by Jan Borman. *Bruges, Church of Notre-Dame.*

teachings of Luther. His edicts against protestant heresy became increasingly severe as his reign went on. But otherwise he had a special affection for the cities of the Netherlands and in particular for Ghent, his birthplace, though this did not prevent him from crushing a popular revolt against his financial exactions in 1539 with brutal promptness. But the wars in which he was constantly embroiled directed his attention elsewhere and tended to shelve the religious issue. It was not until after the abduction of the weary and careworn Emperor at Brussels in 1555 and the accession of his fanatic son, Philip II, that religious persecution became ferocious and not to be borne, leading to the defiance that split the Netherlands in two and the bitter conflict that resulted in the northern United Provinces' declaration of independence in 1579.

The influence of the events of the century on art and artists was various. In the early years under the mild regency of Maximilian's daughter, Margaret of Austria, a peaceful and comparatively prosperous period, court patronage continued much as before, though the style of painting was now somewhat changed by those Italian or 'Romanist' leanings that have been already referred to. Among the artists who worked for her at her palace at Malines, and in Brussels, were such 'Romanists' as Mostaert, Gossaert and Bernard van Orley, who painted her portrait rather in the old Flemish manner. That she knew of and did not disapprove of Bosch is apparent from the fact that two of his paintings hung in her palace.

Quinten Metsys and many other artists in all the more important cities of the

52

53

54

Netherlands were employed on the elaborate decorations that marked the triumphal tour and pageant entries of Charles V on his accession. Though Charles favoured the Venetian rather than the Flemish school – and especially Titian – he and his sister, Maria of Hungary, whom he appointed regent of the Netherlands in succession to Margaret gave much employment to artists. Hundreds of the amazing number that flourished in the first half of the century contributed to the décor of pageantry and 'joyeuses entrées'. They had civic commissions also. Though wool had ceased to be a main source of wealth, trade guilds of another kind, those for example to do with foodstuffs and river navigation, had sprung up and prospered; this is clearly attested by the corporation houses of the Quai aux Herbes at Ghent and their richness of transition from flamboyant Gothic to Renaissance in architectural style (see plate 49). They and the various sporting societies of archers, crossbowmen and fencers kept artists busy on portraits and portrait groups. The picture markets, especially at Antwerp, were as active as ever. Bruges in commercial decay was still mindful of art. The city could commission the grandiose Renaissance fireplace for the council chamber of the Palais du Franc (see plate 55), designed by Lancelot Blondeel (1528–31) with its life-size statues of Maximilian, Mary of Burgundy, Ferdinand and Isabella and Charles V.

There was also a growing interest in local topography. Jan Provoost (1462–1529) made topographic drawings for the Bruges magistracy; Marcus Gheeraerts (c. 1520–c. 1603) made drawings for a plan of Bruges; Pieter Janz Pourbus (c. 1510–1584) not only added background views of its buildings to portraits (as in his 'Jan Fernaguut' where the Place de la Grue appears – a painting in the Bruges Museum, see fig. 29), but also made a panorama of the administrative region known as the *Franc de Bruges* with the aid of sketches taken from the belfry tower.

Some artists were able to take advantage of the international connections of the Habsburgs and the demand for state portraits to travel from court to court and themselves to become international figures. The outstanding example is that of the Utrecht painter, Anthonis Mor (c. 1519–1576), known as Antonio Moro in Spain and (Sir) Anthony More in England. Maria of Hungary commissioned him to go to Portugal to paint her sister Queen Catherine of Portugal and other members of the royal family. He went to England in 1554 on behalf of Philip II to paint Mary Tudor and was then knighted by the Queen. He worked in Spain for Philip and later for the Duke of Alva at Brussels and Antwerp, where he died. Painters, as might be expected, were not in the forefront of religious and political dissension, but they were not immune from the increasing suspicion of heresy in the first half of the 16th century. Bernard van Orley in 1527 was accused, with a number of painters and tapestry workers, of attending protestant sermons. He was acquitted, but others were given the mild penance of hearing the same number of Catholic sermons in St Gudule. Jan Metsys, the painter son of Quinten, was banished in 1544 as a suspected heretic. In 1550 the nervous magistrates of Bruges ordered Pieter Janz Pourbus to paint out the figures of priests whom Jan Provoost had included among the damned in his painting of 'The Last Judgment'.

In the second half of the century the merciless use of the Inquisition, wholesale executions, the arrival of Spanish troops and finally the 'Council of Blood' of the Duke of Alva brought tension to its height. It is against this background that the great figure of Pieter Brueghel the Elder stands out. By far the greatest artist of his time in the Netherlands, he carried to an inspired point developments in painting already on foot, forecast the future course of Dutch and Flemish art and vividly reflected the circumstances of the period. It is assumed that Pieter Brueghel was born at the village of Bruegel in north Brabant, at no great distance from 's-Hertogenbosch about the year 1520. He spent his apprentice years at Antwerp

Fig. 29 Detail of the Place de la Grue from the portrait of Jan Fernaguut by Pieter Pourbus. *Bruges, Groeningemuseum.*

54 'The well of Moses' by Claus Sluter; detail showing Daniel. *Dijon, Chartreuse de Champmol.*

55 Detail of the fireplace in the Council Chamber of the Palais du Franc, Bruges.

56 Fountain attributed to Quinten Metsys in front of the Cathedral, Antwerp.

57 Detail of the façade of the Hôtel de Ville, Ghent.

in the house of Pieter Coecke van Aelst, whose daughter he eventually married. Coecke was a painter and decorative designer (among whose decorative works was the figure of the legendary founder of Antwerp, the giant Antigonus, for the ceremonial entry of Charles V and his son Philip into Antwerp in 1549). Brueghel afterwards worked for Jerome Cock, landscape painter, engraver, print seller and picture dealer who had a prosperous and celebrated shop in Antwerp, 'At the Sign of the Four Winds' (see fig. 1).

Line engravings to suit the popular taste were then in vogue. They included landscapes, prints after Bosch and other artists and illustrations of old saws and pieces of proverbial wisdom. Brueghel's many engravings of this kind had a bearing on the nature of his painting. A full master in the Antwerp Guild, he made the journey to Italy that had become customary, in 1551. But unlike so many of his compatriots he was not at all influenced by Italian art. His art was essentially of his own country in spirit. The journey to Italy seems to have had the principal effect of heightening his awareness of landscape. His first known painting dates from 1558. In the space of eleven years, until his death at Brussels in 1569, he produced the amazing series of masterpieces that proclaim his greatness in imaginative vision, in scenes of popular life, in landscape, in the individual and narrative treatment of biblical history and in reflections of the sombre happenings of his time.

In his paintings of the months, the Gothic calendar of the seasons has evolved at last into landscape superbly combining space, atmosphere and human action. The keen observation of the realist who watched and made sketches from life of peasants at work and play appears in the 'Peasant Dance' and 'The Wedding Feast' (see fig. 32) (Kunsthistorisches Museum, Vienna) and again in 'The Fall of Icarus' (Brussels, Musées Royaux des Beaux Arts, see plate 61) in which mythology becomes an excuse for one of his most romantic visions. His sense of reality gave contemporary point to subjects in which he followed Bosch in satire and pictorial parable. 'The Triumph of Death' (Prado—see plates 64 & 65) is a parallel with Bosch's 'Hay Wain' in its conception of the fate that awaits every class of society. But in addition to the parable there is such a view of fire and slaughter, burning buildings and sinking ships as seems to convey his comment on the tragic state of the Netherlands under Spanish rule.

Brueghel moved from Antwerp to Brussels in 1563. His mother-in-law stipulated that he should thus sever a connection with a former mistress. Brussels also had advantages as court centre and Habsburg capital. His work found imperial favour, a reason why so many of his paintings are preserved at Vienna. It was Brussels which in 1567 was the headquarters of the cruel Duke of Alva, sworn to stamp out heresy with fire and sword, full of Spanish troops. The protests of leading citizens against the inquisitorial courts had been contemptuously rejected as those of 'a troop of beggars' (*gueux*) – a title defiantly adopted by the forces of the resistance. One of Alva's first acts was the execution of the Counts Egmont and Hoorn in the Brussels market-place. It is impossible not to suppose that Brueghel's sympathies were with the rebellious nationalists and reformers. It is recorded by the artist-historian, van Mander, that on his deathbed he ordered the destruction of drawings on which he had written bitter remarks, that if left and discovered might have brought trouble to his wife. But in paintings to be seen by others the comment was hidden or cryptically implicit in the theme and its treatment. 'The Massacre of the Innocents' (Vienna), ostensibly an illustration of Bible history, represents a typical snow-bound village of Brueghel's time, terrorized by troops with all the appearance of imperial mercenaries. 'The Census of Bethlehem' (Brussels) suggests the grim investigation of the emissaries of Philip II rather than of Herod (see plate 91). Brueghel's last picture 'The Magpie on the Gibbet' places dancing peasants near to a waiting

Fig. 30 Portrait of Hubert Goltzius by Antony More, 1576. *Brussels, Musées Royaux des Beaux Arts.*

58 'The banker and his wife' by Quinten Metsys, 1514. (28 × 27in., 70 × 67.5cm.) *Paris, Musée du Louvre.*

59 Detail of the right background of the central panel of the 'Baptism of Christ' by Gerard David, 1502–3. *Bruges, Groeningemuseum.* (See also plate 74)

60 Detail of vases of flowers from 'The Adoration of the Shepherds' (Portinari Altarpiece) by Hugo van der Goes, c. 1475. *Florence, Uffizi Gallery.* (See also plate 20)

61 'The Fall of Icarus' by Pieter Brueghel, c. 1553. (29 × 44in., 72.5 × 110.3cm.) *Brussels, Musées Royaux des Beaux Arts.*

58

Fig. 31 Portrait of C. Plantin,
engraved by H. Goltzius.
*Antwerp, Museum
Plantin-Moretus.*

62 Detail of the Good Thief
and the Dominican from 'The
Bearing of the Cross' by
Hieronymus Bosch, c. 1505.
Ghent, Musée des Beaux Arts.
(See also plate 73)

63 Detail from 'Heaven', the
left panel of 'The Garden of
Terrestrial Delights' by
Hieronymus Bosch, c. 1503.
(Whole triptych 77 × 86½in.,
192.5 × 216.3cm.) *Madrid,
Museo del Prado.* (See also plate 66)

64 Detail from 'The Triumph
of Death' by Pieter Brueghel,
c. 1560. (Whole painting
46½ × 63¾in., 115.3 × 159.4cm.)
Madrid, Museo del Prado.

65 Detail of a boat with
skeletons from 'The Triumph
of Death' by Pieter Brueghel.
Madrid, Museo del Prado.

scaffold. He left it to his wife as a warning against dangerous talk.

At the time of Brueghel's death there was general chaos. In both the North and South of the Netherlands there were iconoclastic outbreaks that despoiled monastic houses and shattered the sculpture and defaced the paintings of churches. They met with fierce reprisal. The cities suffered as much from indiscriminate pillage by Alva's soldiers as from penalties officially ordered. Antwerp, the great centre of learning and commerce, that had been the pride of Charles V, was brought low by the 'Spanish Fury' of 1576 when an army mutinous at being unpaid, looted the city, in the process massacring 7,000 citizens, destroying 1,000 buildings and burning down the Hôtel de Ville. Alva completed its commercial ruin by the crippling sales tax known as the *Dixième Denier*.

In the years of bitter fighting that followed, ending with the union of the northern provinces in 1579 and their renunciation of allegiance to Spain in 1584, artists were among the many displaced. Some went northwards to Holland to unite themselves with the patriotic party or to gain the comparative safety of the provinces under William of Orange. There were families among them with children who in time became Dutch painters in an independent Holland, such as the landscape and still-life painter, Roelandt Savery of Courtrai, the flower painter Ambrosius Bosschaert of Antwerp, the landscape and animal painter Gillis de Hondecoeter, whose son and grandson were to be well known as Dutch bird painters. Numerous artists were in the great exodus abroad of 100,000 protestant and other refugees. Some went to England where Flemish painters and craftsmen had found earlier welcome. An arrival in London before the 'fury' was well under way, in about 1545 was Hans Eworth, of Antwerp, who found employment as portrait painter and designer of masques and allegories at the Elizabethan court and died, probably in London, towards the end of the century. The later emigrants included the painter and designer, Marcus Gheeraerts the Elder of Bruges (c. 1520–c. 1603) who after being employed on such work in Bruges churches as decorative additions to the tombs of Charles the Bold and Mary of Burgundy fled from Alva's régime to London in 1568. He brought with him his seven-year-old son, Marcus the Younger (1561–1635) who became portrait painter to Queen Elizabeth and James I. Others went to Germany and some wandered from place to place. Joris Hoefnagel, miniature painter, illustrator and engraver (1542–1600), the son of a diamond merchant at Antwerp, left the city in 1576 and worked in Augsburg, Venice, Rome, Naples, Munich and finally at Vienna where he died. Cornelis Ketel of Gouda (1548–1616), expelled from France with other Netherlandish immigrants in 1566, afterwards went to London where he painted portraits but returned to Holland in 1581 and settled at Amsterdam.

The great Antwerp printing house of Christophe Plantin (1514–1589) where between 1568 and 1573 he published his Polyglot Bible in eight volumes, called the *Biblia Regia* in honour of Philip II, did not escape the undiscriminating destruction of 1576. It suffered from fire and though the business did not close down, Plantin himself left the city to work for some years at Leiden. Plantin's assistant, Louis Elzevir of Louvain (1540–1618), a Calvinist and so with the more reason to fly from Antwerp, also settled at Leiden to found the Dutch publishing house which was long to rival that of Plantin in the beauty and educational importance of its productions.

After the recall of Alva and the final subjugation of the southern cities by the capable soldier, Alessandro Farnese, Duke of Parma, the scene of confused and complicated movement simplifies itself. On the one hand is a triumphant, patriotically united and strongly protestant Holland; on the other the southern provinces from which the protestant element has been all but extirpated, subject in religious

matters to the activity of the Jesuits and ruled from Brussels by a Spanish court.
The great age of Dutch maritime and overseas expansion was to begin bringing an
unprecedented prosperity to the ports of Amsterdam and Rotterdam, giving them
the advantage over Antwerp. In the arts the single stem of former times now had
divergent branches. Both were to blossom richly in the age to come.

Fig. 32   Detail from 'The Wedding Feast' by Pieter Brueghel.
(Whole painting $44\frac{7}{8} \times 64\frac{1}{8}$in., 114×163cm.) *Vienna,
Kunsthistorisches Museum.*

Fig. 33   Design for Triumphal Car by Rubens. (40½ × 28½in., 101.3 × 71.3cm.) *Antwerp, Musée Royal des Beaux Arts.*

In the early 17th century under the peaceable rule of Archduke Albert ('the Pious') of Austria and his wife, the Infanta Isabella, tranquillity and a measure of prosperity returned by degrees to the Flemish cities. They showed their traditional resilience. Brussels became a gay capital with its court masques and balls and outdoor fêtes, processions and pageants. Frans Francken painted the formal court dance in the Spanish fashion when one couple at a time performed with stiffly ceremonious steps. Denis van Alsloot made a series of pictures for the Archduchess of the *Ommeganck* procession held in her honour in 1615, with its ornamental horse-drawn floats carrying their complement of girls in symbolic attire (see fig. 34).

Antwerp again became busy as a port, in spite of Dutch rivalry, having its share of trade with America and the Far East. It held its own until by the terms of the Treaty of Münster that ended the Thirty Years War in 1648 the Scheldt was closed to trade. This concession of Spain to Holland dealt Antwerp a crippling blow. Bruges and Ghent had suffered heavily in the religious and civil strife from the operations of both sides. Ghent was able to revive her traffic along the inland waterways but Bruges at the end of the 16th century was in a sad plight. It had been occupied for six years by the 'Sea Beggars' who established their own reign of terror, looting the city's treasure, executing or driving into exile the clergy. The wealthy burghers had gone long before, the city was depopulated. Yet there was now a revival of a sort.

Fig. 34   Detail from Isabella's Triumph in the *Ommeganck* by Denis van Alsloot. (Whole painting 46 × 150in., 115 × 375cm.) *London, Victoria and Albert Museum. Crown Copyright.*

Fig. 35 Portrait of Justus Lipsius, drawing by Rubens. *London, British Museum.*

66 Detail from 'Hell', right panel of 'The Garden of Terrestrial Delights' by Hieronymus Bosch. *Madrid, Museo del Prado.* (See also plate 63)

67 Detail of the Boar Hunt from 'The Devonshire Hunting Tapestries'. *London, Victoria and Albert Museum.*

In the country around Bruges and Ghent many monastic houses had been destroyed. By a strange turn of fate this became to Bruges's advantage. The monks and nuns flocked into the city. They had managed to salvage a good deal of their portable wealth and artistic property. Churches and monasteries were restored, new dwellings and buildings devoted to good works erected. The unpretentious *Godshuisen* or almshouses added a new picturesqueness to the city's aspect (see plates 2 & 90). Bruges gained that appearance and atmosphere of monastic seclusion and quiet that has distinguished it ever since.

Religious discipline in the southern provinces as a whole was strict but not, it would seem, oppressive. Indeed except for a few Lutherans or Calvinists, no longer a danger and regarded as eccentrics to be tolerated, the provinces numbered only adherents of the old faith or those without strong convictions who were ready to accept it. The Jesuits were dominant and with Jesuitism came the baroque style of architecture, sculpture and painting, the art of the Counter-Reformation, a visual and propagandist expression of the renewed energy of Church and absolutist state. The church of St Jean Baptiste au Béguinage at Brussels, built in the mid-17th century to the design of the architect and sculptor, Luc Fayd'herbe of Malines, with its florid volutes, broken pediments and sculptural façade perfectly exemplifies the baroque of Jesuit Rome. In contrast with the Gothic choir of St Gudule were the theatrically baroque statues of the Apostles introduced into the interior in the 17th century. Sculptors such as Artus Quellin (1609–1668) and François du Quesnoy (c. 1594–1643) worked in Rome for a while and derived their style from the great exponent of the baroque in sculpture, Lorenzo Bernini. The baroque in painting had its supreme northern representative in Peter Paul Rubens.

The differences – and still some likenesses – of Dutch and Flemish art in the 17th century make a fascinating study. The interior of a church in Holland, denuded of any papist symbol, was a spectacle of puritan austerity, and, as shown in the work of the Dutch artist, Saenredam, had none of the profusion of paintings and ornament that persisted in the south. Iconoclasm had so far done its work that little evidence of the early Dutch aptitude for sculpture remained. Painting with a liturgical function also disappeared from Holland; in the Catholic south it was practised as actively as ever. The wealthy Dutch bourgeois was no longer a pious donor portrayed in an altarpiece but one whose secular importance is reflected in portraiture. A contrast can be drawn between Rembrandt's translation of biblical incident into terms of everyday humanity and such a prodigious composition by Rubens, testifying to Catholic fervour, as 'The Miracle of St Ignatius Loyola' painted for the altar of the Jesuit Church at Antwerp.

Dutch artists were nationalists whose efforts were directed to giving a portrait of their country in its flush of victory and independence, its companies of civic guards, its middle class at home, its typical flat landscape. The Flemish, working for foreign rulers and nobles, were more internationally minded. Differences of temperament in earlier days obscured by the intercommunication in the arts of cities, North and South, now became more clearly marked. Yet the two Netherlands still showed qualities in common when it came to painting scenes of popular life and the flower and still-life pictures in which the 17th century was prolific.

The first half of the 17th century was Antwerp's great period as a centre of art. Brussels was admired as one of the largest and finest cities in Europe as well as for the glamour attaching to the court but Antwerp was the intellectual and creative centre. It was the city of Rubens, whose genius, as distinctively Flemish as that of Rembrandt was Dutch, dominated the period. Little could his great and uniformly fortunate career be foretold from the circumstances of his early childhood. His father, Jan Rubens, contrived to get on the wrong side of both the opposing parties.

66

A lawyer and alderman at Antwerp of protestant sympathies, he was suspected of Calvinism during the Alva régime and escaped with his wife to Cologne in 1568. An affair with the wife of William of Orange, the Princess of Saxony, led to his imprisonment at Cologne and afterwards to his detention at Siegen in Westphalia, where Peter Paul Rubens was born in 1577. When his father died ten years later, his mother who had resumed the Catholic faith, took him back to Antwerp, where he added a sound classical education to what he had learned under her care in Germany.

68 'Adam and Eve' by Jan
Brueghel and Rubens, 1615–20.
(30 × 61in., 75 × 152.5cm.)
*The Hague, Koninklijk Kabinet
van Schilderijen, Mauritshuis.*

Fig. 36   'The Raising of the Cross' by Rubens, 1612–14. Centre
panel of a triptych. (165½ × 122in., 414 × 305cm.) *Antwerp, the Cathedral.*

As a boy of fourteen, made a page to the widow of Count Philip of Lalaing, he must have gained a useful introduction to the modes and manners of aristocratic life. As a student of painting he was able to sample the methods of three Antwerp masters, first the landscape painter, Tobias van Hecht, then the painter of religious subjects, Adam van Noort, finally Otto van Veen, court painter to the Archduke Albert and his wife. Van Veen probably recommended the young man to his patrons. Through them he was introduced to Vincenzo Gonzaga, Duke of Mantua, who made Rubens his court painter. At the age of twenty-three he was brilliantly launched.

A stay of eight years in Italy, including a visit to Spain, rounded off his education in art. He studied classical sculpture, copied the Italian Renaissance masters both for the Duke of Mantua and for his own instruction, and was able to observe the contemporary movement of art in Italy from mannerism to baroque. On his return to Antwerp in 1608, a mature painter, cosmopolitan in experience and giant in ability, he found immediate welcome. The commissions for paintings asserting the authority of Catholicism poured in. Pupils flocked to him. They were essential to complete the vast number of requests that came both from home and abroad. Of his religious compositions for Flemish churches some are still *in situ*. Two famous examples are the masterpieces in Antwerp Cathedral, 'The Raising of the Cross' (1610–11) with its straining diagonal movement, 'The Descent from the Cross' (1611–14) with its sad, drooping curves (see plate 85 & fig. 36). For Notre-Dame, Malines, he executed one of his triumphs of figure painting, 'The Miraculous Draught of Fishes' (1617). A number of the paintings for churches at Antwerp, Brussels, Ghent are now in the Belgian museums, among them the renowned 'Coup de Lance' painted in 1620 for the Church of the Recollects (Antwerp Museum, see plate 71).

The range of Rubens's painting has never ceased to arouse astonishment. He invested every form of secular subject with his tremendous power: allegory, mythology, portraiture, landscape, even the peasant genre. Of his own life his paintings give their vivid chronicle. We see him 'in the honeysuckle arbour', with his first wife, Isabella Brant about the time of their marriage in 1610, the dress of each so beautifully detailed (including collar and ruff of fine Flemish lace) in the picture now at Munich, that the student of 17th-century fashion could ask for no better guide (Alte Pinakothek, Munich, see plate 96). His pride in the house he then bought is suggested at a later date by his picture of the garden and ornate pavilion towards which he and his young second wife, Hélène Fourment, are seen strolling. In 1635 his purchase of a country mansion in the neighbourhood of Malines inspired him to produce the great landscapes of the Flemish countryside of his later years. The beautiful cathedral of Malines has been discerned in the distance in his 'Evening Return from the Fields at Mowing Time' (Pitti Palace, Florence). The house itself, the Château de Steen, as it appeared on an autumn day is seen in the great landscape in the National Gallery, London (see plate 70).

There was no form of design on which he did not exert an influence. He advised on the architecture of the Jesuit church at Antwerp, and various features of his own house were added to his design. The magnificent baroque portico by which his studio was approached reflected his familiarity with Italian architecture (see plates 88 & 89). He could invent such a grandiose combination of arches, perspectives, sculptured ornament and painted detail as was required for the state entry of the Cardinal Infante Ferdinand into Antwerp in 1635 (see fig. 33). The craft of tapestry weaving at Brussels which had begun to decline gained a temporary revival in carrying out the commissions for tapestry design that came to him from abroad. He gave a new stimulus to engraving and book-illustration of which

Fig. 37   Two figures in early medieval costume, drawn by Rubens from the tomb of Louis de Maele at Lille, now disappeared. From *Rubens Costume Book*. London, *British Museum*.

Antwerp had long been a centre. Plantin's publications were celebrated for their beauty of type and the engraved illustrations of which he made much use. The designs Rubens made for the inheritors of the firm, especially for title-pages engraved on copper, gave fresh prestige to the books produced by the Plantin press. A European demand for engraved reproductions of his paintings kept a whole school of engravers busy under his supervision, which was exacting. They seem often to have worked from his grisaille sketches rather than finished paintings but Rubens demanded a fullness of light and shade and modelling that approximated to his own. Such engravers as Schelte Adams Bolswert (c. 1586–1659), Lucas Vorsterman (1595–c. 1675), Jonas Suydergoef (c. 1610–86) and Paul Pontius (1603–38) brought the translations of tone into line to a new pitch of perfection. As a draughtsman also he ranks with the greatest masters of the Renaissance (see figs. 35 & 37).

Handsome, courtly of manners, intellectually gifted and an accomplished linguist, Rubens was well fitted for the diplomatic rôle with which he was entrusted by the Infanta Isabella, successfully conducting the secret negotiations that took him on journeys to Paris and London, Madrid and Amsterdam. These unusual responsibilities also produced important commissions: the twenty-one panels of 'The History of Marie de' Medici' for the Luxembourg Palace; the ceiling of the Banqueting House, Whitehall, for Charles I. For Charles also he worked as a diplomat, and as adviser on his magnificent collection of pictures (he arranged for the sale of the Mantua collection to London), for all of which he was rewarded with a knighthood. His huge output necessarily demanded an army of collaborators, assistants and pupils. His great studio, some 45 by 35 feet in size and the additional workshops above it formed a picture-factory where he had the aid of such brilliant artists as Jordaens, Snyders, Jan Brueghel and van Dyck.

Antoon van Dijck – by English title and description, Sir Anthony van Dyck – before the long stay in England, from 1632 to 1641 (the year of his death at Black-friars) which gives him his illustrious place in the development of the English school of portraiture, came near to Rubens as a Flemish master of the baroque. The son of a silk-merchant at Antwerp and born there in 1599, he was a pupil of the painter of religious themes and landscapes, Hendrik van Balen (1575–1632). He became Rubens's assistant at the age of nineteen, though his subsequent stay in Italy, where he painted portraits and studied both the portraiture of Titian and baroque religious painting, helped him to form his style independently. On his return to Antwerp he had his own studio and painted the superb compositions for churches in which he rivals Rubens. A masterpiece of this kind is 'The Ecstasy of St Augustine' in the church of St Augustine at Antwerp (see plate 84) where it vies with Rubens's 'The Betrothal of St Catherine'. But such works represent only one phase of his career. He was more amenable than Rubens to the suggestion of settling in England and more responsive to a change of environment. The spirit of Antwerp in art was vigorous and robust to the point of coarseness. In England the painting of van Dyck took on a refinement and even a certain melancholy that seem to reflect the mood of the Stuart court.

Others who worked more closely and for a longer period with Rubens display one or other facets of his style without approaching him in many-sidedness. Jacob Jordaens (1593–1678) had much of Rubens's facility though in a coarser vein. Yet he painted the Flemish types that appear in both genre scenes and allegories with great vivacity and understanding. Frans Snyders (1579–1657), son of the tavern keeper of the 'Groote Bruyloft Kamere' (an Antwerp artists' resort) worked with Rubens as a skilled specialist in animal painting and still-life. That universal master anticipated the Romantics of the early 19th century in picturing unleashed animal violence and power, as in his paintings of the lion hunt and boar hunt. In scenes

Fig. 38   Portrait of Cornelius van der Geest by Anthony van Dyck. The sitter, who died in 1638, was an Antwerp merchant, art collector and friend of Rubens. (14¾ × 12¾in., 36.9 × 31.9cm.) *London, National Gallery.*

Fig. 39   Detail from Still Life No. 336 by Frans Snyders. (Whole painting 46 × 81in., 115 × 202.8cm.) *Antwerp, Musée Royal des Beaux Arts.*

Fig. 40   Detail from 'The Card Game' by Adriaen Brouwer. (Whole painting 10 × 15¾in., 25 × 39.4cm.) *Antwerp, Musée Royal des Beaux Arts.*

Fig. 41   The Drinkers by David Teniers the younger. (15 × 19¾in., 37.5 × 48.3cm.) *Antwerp, Musée Royal des Beaux Arts.*

69   Detail from the Altarpiece by Rubens in the chapel with his tomb, c. 1626. (193 × 128in., 465.5 × 323.3cm.) *Antwerp, Church of Saint Jacques.*

70   'Château de Steen' by Rubens, c. 1636. (54 × 92½in., 137 × 234cm.) *London, National Gallery.*

of this kind Snyders excelled. In his still-lifes, often depicting heaps of game, he showed a characteristically Flemish delight in abundance (see fig. 39). Though the northern and southern Netherlands shared pleasure in the material richness of still-life objects, it is possible to contrast the lavish painting of the trophies of aristocratic sport with that of the good things of the Dutch table and its propriety of china and glass.

In the same way it is possible to distinguish between the pictures of social life, North and South. The Dutch convey the decorum of a protestant middle class for the most part, though there are exceptions such as the roistering scenes of Jan Steen and the jolly bohemians Frans Hals liked to paint as a relief from the formal commission. In the South there remained the greater extremes of a society in which the noble and the peasant were complementary. Rubens could encompass both, the aristocratic idyll of the 'Garden of Love' (Prado), the peasant dance of the 'Kermesse' (Louvre) (see plates 95 & 97). Some artists specialized in pictures that reflected the wealth and taste of the nobility as exemplified in their picture galleries. Frans Francken the younger (1581–1642), and Willem van Haecht (1593–1637) are among a number of Antwerp artists who painted interiors of this kind.

Peasant life was the study of those with a freer social comment to make. Adriaen Brouwer (c. 1605–38), born at Audenarde but trained in Haarlem where he was a pupil of Frans Hals and belonging to Antwerp by adoption, is a great example. His early work followed Brueghel in brightness of colour but later he discards this gaiety of scheme to concentrate on stark reality. Brueghel was inimitable in his humorous observation of Flemish rustic types and the liveliness and movement of the special occasions when they turned out in their best to dance on the village green to the drone of bagpipes or to feast at the long trestle table of the wedding banquet from the array of dishes brought in on a rough wooden stretcher. Rubens gave a less particularized, even a classical, character to his painting of a Flemish Kermesse. It was left for Brouwer to convey the drab and sordid atmosphere of drinking dens, dark and bare, their air impregnated with the stale odours of ale, tobacco and humanity (see fig. 40).

Yet Brouwer as an artist was not drab or sordid. His unsentimental vision, appreciative sometimes of low comedy, had the seriousness of a great painter. Rubens and Rembrandt discerned it and both acquired a number of his pictures. In this genre North and South were in accord. Flemish and Dutch painters alike followed Brouwer in scenes of low life. Adriaen van Ostade (1610–85) provides a parallel in Holland though without the same tension of effect. Joos van Craesbeek, baker at the prison in Antwerp Castle who met Brouwer when he was confined there in 1633, turned painter as a result. He became Brouwer's companion in revelry and imitator in such works as his picture of a tavern brawl 'At the Antwerp Arms' (Antwerp Museum). Brouwer's most original follower was the prolific and successful David Teniers the younger (1610–90). Tavern and village scenes (see fig. 41) are numerous among the 2,000 pictures with which he is credited, alternating with the eccentric fancies of his paintings of alchemy, witchcraft and saintly temptation.

It may be doubted whether any city at any time has had as many artists as Antwerp in the 17th century. They were certainly more numerous there than in any other city of the southern Netherlands. Some came from elsewhere but the majority were Antwerp-born. Sons tended to follow fathers in the flourishing industry of painting. Artist families often intermarried. An extraordinary number of family dynasties of art is to be found. They answered to a constant demand; from the Church in its renewed energy, the court, the municipality, the merchant community, and from patrons in other countries where the prestige of Flemish art stood high.

The family tradition and practice of art made for consistent standards of craft

69

and gave Antwerp many of the highly accomplished minor masters of the time. As it happened none of Rubens's four sons became a painter nor did any of his three daughters marry an artist, though in a sense he might be said to stand in a paternal relation to the pupils of his picture factory. But there were five painter-members of the Teniers family in addition to David Teniers the younger. There were three generations of the de Vos family of whom the best known is the portrait painter, Cornelis de Vos (1585–1651) (see plate 83). The Floris (de Vriendt) family produced sculptors and painters. The Quellins, the Franckens, the Kessels are further examples. The most remarkable dynasty of all was that of the Brueghel family, its history in art extending over 300 years and counting in all no fewer than twenty-six painters.

The genius of Pieter Brueghel the Elder was a quality that could not be inherited, but critics have sometimes been unnecessarily severe in their estimate of his two sons, Pieter the Younger (1564–1638) and Jan Brueghel I (1568–1625), after him the family's principal representatives in the 17th century. Pieter the Younger is best known as one who made copies and variations of the Elder's themes, understandably without the latter's power but in a naive style not without its own attraction. His nickname 'Hell' refers to his copies of such paintings as 'The Triumph of Death' though the remaining products of his industry are more often scenes of peasant life. He appears of distinguished aspect with pointed beard and elaborate ruff in van Dyck's 'Iconography' of his contemporaries. A far more original and sensitive artist was his brother Jan, nicknamed 'Velvet' on account of his liking for finery in dress (though the suavity of his painting might also be so described). Though he collaborated with Rubens (see plate 68) and shared with him the favour of Archduke Albert and his wife he represents a different aspect of Flemish art, in no way connected with the baroque tradition. He was eminent among the painters who depicted landscape with something of the miniaturist's delicacy; also in the development of flower painting as a distinct genre.

The love of nature in the form of landscape and flowers had always been evident in Netherlandish art. The masters of the 15th century had found a release of the imagination in devising the vistas of river country that served as background for Madonna and donor. The practice that became usual in the 16th century of journeying to Italy for study added the impression made by mountains to their repertoire of landscape forms. The elder Brueghel in his great painting 'January' (Kunsthistorisches Museum, Vienna, see fig. 44) combines the flat country of the Netherlands with a distant view of Alpine heights (these appear again in the drawing now in the Pierpont Morgan Library, New York, see fig. 45). A number of minor masters in the late 16th and early 17th century give this half-realistic, half-imaginative impression of travel – such Antwerp painters for instance as Gillis van Coninxloo (1544–1607), Joos (Jodocus) de Momper (1564–1635) and Paul Bril (c. 1554–1626). Bril settled in Italy and his paintings of rocky and wooded landscapes with Roman ruins, showing the romantic influence of Italy on the northern mind (as on that of his German contemporary, Adam Elsheimer) were in part instrumental in creating the special genre of 'classical' landscape.

In combining the imaginative and the minute Jan Brueghel was akin to these Antwerp contemporaries. He has a relation also with the flower and still-life painters whose work evolved from old tradition. A large number of flowers and plants exquisitely detailed and botanically recognizable, appear in the religious compositions of the 15th-century masters. The epitaph of Jan van Eyck notes how he adorned the painted ground with 'florentibus herbis'. Memlinc painted centaury, marguerite and ragged robin with an obvious affection. Saxifrage, poppy, cinquefoil and clematis are to be found in the paintings of van der Weyden. Flowers

Fig. 42   Detail from the portrait of Ignatius de Loyola by Daniel Seghers. (116½ × 75in., 291.6 × 187.5cm.) *Antwerp, Musée Royal des Beaux Arts.*

Fig. 43   Vase of Flowers by Jan Brueghel. (18⅝ × 14in., 47 × 35cm.) *Madrid, Museo del Prado.*

71   Crucifixion – 'Coup de Lance' by Rubens, 1620. (156¼ × 117in., 429 × 311cm.) *Antwerp, Musée Royal des Beaux Arts.*

72 'The Arrest of the Corrupt Judge' by Gerard David. Companion to 'The Justice of Cambyses', 1498–9. (72 × 62½in., 180 × 156.3cm.) *Bruges, Groeningemuseum.*

73 'The Bearing of the Cross' by Hieronymus Bosch, c. 1505. (30¾ × 33¼in., 76.7 × 83.5cm.) *Ghent, Musée des Beaux Arts.* (See also plate 62)

74 'The Baptism of Christ' by Gerard David, 1502–3. Jan van Tromp, burgomaster of Bruges in 1501, is shown accompanied by his son and presented by Saint John the Evangelist, in the left hand panel. The right hand panel shows his first wife Elizabeth van der Meersch, presented by Elizabeth of Hungary, who is accompanied by her four daughters. (51 × 77in., 127.5 × 192.5cm.) *Bruges, Groeningemuseum.* (See also plate 59)

75 'Flight into Egypt' by Joachim Patinir. (6¾ × 8½in., 17 × 21cm.) *Antwerp, Musée Royal des Beaux Arts.*

76 'Saint Jerome in a rocky landscape' by Joachim Patinir. (14¼ × 13½in., 36.5 × 34cm.) *London, National Gallery.*

77 'Death of the Virgin' by Hugo van der Goes, c. 1470. (58½ × 48in., 146 × 120cm.) *Bruges, Groeningemuseum.*

78 'The Seven Griefs of Mary' by A. Ysenbrandt, c. 1510. (55 × 55in., 138 × 138cm.) *Bruges, Notre-Dame.* (See also plate 80)

79 Portrait of Edward Grimston by Petrus Christus, 1446. (12½ × 9⅛in., 23 × 31cm.) *St Albans, The Gorhambury Collection.*

Fig. 44 'January' or 'Hunters in the Snow' by Pieter Brueghel, 1565. (46 × 63¾in., 117 × 162cm.) *Vienna, Kunsthistorisches Museum.*

Fig. 45 Detail of mountain landscape, drawing by Pieter Brueghel. *New York, Pierpont Morgan Library.*

had a symbolic meaning which they long retained. In numerous Annunciations a vase of flowers tells of the virtues of the Madonna, the lily representing purity, the iris, majesty, the columbine, motherly love. In 16th-century portraits the sitter often holds a pink, a flower which may have been the symbol of engagement or marriage but was also credited with the property of warding off disease. In the 17th century flowers became a feature of the allegories which then had a popular

73

74

75

76

82

83

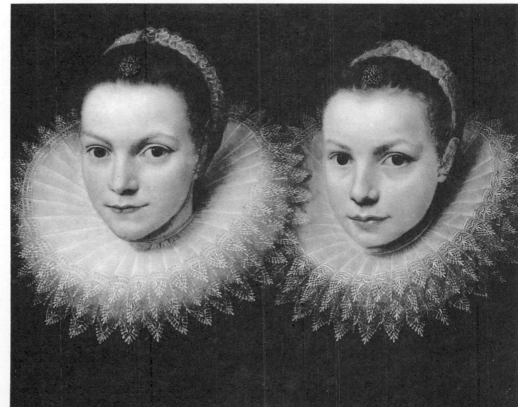

86

vogue, such as 'The Four Elements' in which they symbolized Earth and 'The Five Senses' in which they stood for Smell. They represent the fragile and fleeting nature of beauty or of human life in general in the *Vanitas* paintings also characteristic of the age. The Antwerp painter, Nicolas van Verendael (1640–91) for example paints columbine and campanula beside a burnt-out candle and a grinning skull.

Flower painting in a purely realistic manner was especially cultivated at Antwerp. A new interest was aroused by the botanists whose works the house of Plantin published, and the delicate engraved illustrations accompanying them. Rarities came to Antwerp by sea and were transplanted by the Flemish horticulturists. In the 16th century the tulip was brought from Adrianople by the Emperor Ferdinand's ambassador to the sultan Soliman. It was taken northwards into Holland by refugees from the Spanish reign of terror. The production of different varieties which became a 'tulipomania' both in Holland and the southern Netherlands created a demand for pictures portraying them that occupied artists in both regions. Jan Brueghel stands out among the Flemish landscape and flower painters by the beautiful refinement of his style and the variety he was able to introduce. Such a painting as the 'Adam and Eve' of *c.* 1620 (Mauritshuis, The Hague) in which Rubens collaborated with him, adding the figures, reveals an unexpected harmony between Rubens's largeness of style and the poetic fancy with which Brueghel fills his Garden of Eden with animals and birds of every description (see plate 68). No doubt he studied lion and tiger, camel and ostrich, peacock and parakeet in the Imperial Menagerie at Brussels.

The fashion of the time wreathed a type of devotional painting with a floral garland, a development perhaps suggested by the relation between border and miniature in the illuminated manuscript. Rubens again collaborated with Brueghel in a superb example, 'The Virgin with a Garland' (Louvre). It was the finest thing he had ever done, Brueghel wrote to his patron Cardinal Borromeo, when sending him the picture. 'Le Sieur Rubens', he added, had painted a very beautiful Madonna. He himself had painted the birds and animals from those in the Infanta's possession. The garlanded picture became the speciality of Jan Brueghel's pupil, the Jesuit, Daniel Seghers (1590-1661). He wreaths the portrait of Ignatius de Loyola (Antwerp Museum) with extravagant decoration. Brueghel set the style of painting vases of flowers, brilliantly coloured against a dark background which became a feature of the century's art in the Netherlands generally. Jan Brueghel's grandson, Abraham (1631–90) carried the genre abroad – to Naples where he settled in 1672, with some effect on the outlook and productions of the Neapolitan school.

Flemish art also provides material for the history of the garden. From the trim rectangular flower beds and the grassy walk by the battlements in the background of the 'Madonna and Female Donor' by the Master of St Gudule it can be seen how the city walls were made into a kind of pleasance. The rose garden with its low wall and trellis was an intimate enclosure in the 15th century in which artists would place the Madonna in contemplation. To such a garden the Bruges painter and architect, Jan Provoost (1462–1529) adds a Gothic fountain, in a picture acquired by the Cardinal Giulio Alberoni on a visit to Flanders and now in the Collegio Alberoni, Piacenza. In the 16th century the garden of the palace and noble mansion was enlarged and laid out with the geometric formality that appears in the work of the painter and garden architect, Hans Vredeman de Vries (1527–*c.* 1604). Denis van Alsloot conveys the severely formal layout of the grounds of the archducal château of Mariemont. Garden design often provided separate enclosures for archery and other sports. A drawing by J. Wildens formerly attributed to Frederic van Valckenborgh (1570–1623) in the Rijksprentenkabinet, Amsterdam, shows a game of bowls in progress in one such park enclosure. Often spectacular use was made of architectural features in the Italian style. Lucas van Uden (1595–1672) gives an example in a painting of the belvedere in the garden of Bishop Triest at Ghent (Byloke Museum, Ghent). Terraces, summerhouses and fountains, playfully designed to spray the arriving guests, take on a fanciful aspect in a painting by Sebastian Vranckx (1573–1647) of an Italianate palace, preserved in Rubens's house at Antwerp (see fig. 46). The fête champêtre, however, as depicted by such painters of the aristocratic environment as Lucas van Valckenborgh (c. 1530–97) and David Vinckeboons (1576–1632) seems conducted with a gravity that matches the Spanish stateliness of fashion in the dress of the participants.

The first half of the 17th century marks the zenith of the Flemish achievement in the arts. Rubens died in 1640. As Bruges had declined with the closing of the Zwijn so now did Antwerp with the closing of the Scheldt ordained by the Treaty of Münster in 1648. It was the turn of Holland from then on to take over commercial supremacy and at the same time to enjoy its own golden age of art. Yet the influence of the great Rubens, not confined to his own city and time, was a dynamic force that gave wave on wave of inspiration to Europe; to the Neapolitan school towards the end of the 17th century – Luca Giordano derived energy and movement from him; to the French painters of the 18th century – Watteau's fêtes champêtres emerge from Rubens's 'Garden of Love'. Boucher and Fragonard too are beneficiaries of what was known in their time as *Rubénisme*. He is the precursor of the Romantics, Géricault and Delacroix, who emulate his expression of the violence of nature in scenes of battle and the chase. As the nerve centre of Europe, drawing together the impulses of North and South, the Netherlands had in him a prodigious personal concentration and legacy to leave.

Fig. 46   Painting of an Italianate Palace by Sebastian Vranckx.
(23¼ × 34in., 58.3 × 85cm.) *Antwerp, Rubens's House.*

There is no more extraordinary survival from the Flemish past than Bruges. For generations it has cast its spell over the poet, the mystic, the lover of art, the antiquary, the visitor more simply in search of the picturesque. Considered in a purely aesthetic light it is a city of exceptional beauty. The mellowness of brick which is a special feature of its architecture gives it a consistent but varied harmony of colour from a deep russet red to a pale ochre. The canals that wind round and through the city present a diversity of compositions in which walls, bridges and water are delightfully related. There is a superb focus of interest in the great belfry that rises to a height of 350 feet above the medieval market hall and above the great square of the city, commanding from its summit the panorama and intricate array of steep-pitched roofs and stepped gables (see plate 8).

The canals, as at Amsterdam, have made for the usual comparisons with Venice, though they are of a somewhat superficial kind, but the noble proportions of the Grand'Place, the more impressive in contrast with the narrow ways that converge upon it and from which it suddenly expands, may well bring to mind the effect of the Venetian Piazza di San Marco. Yet the impression of beauty is inevitably linked with many associations, the feeling of time suspended, of a history that at some time in the past reached its close.

It is the atmosphere that pervades the course of the inner canals that mark the perimeter of the earliest city walls before the outward expansion of medieval times; the Dyver, the Quai du Rosaire, the Quai des Marbriers (see plate 11), the Quai Vert, the Quai aux Herbes (see plate 3). It is the gentle melancholy that tinges the elegiac prospect of the Minnewater or 'Lake of Love', swan-haunted, shaded by weeping willows with its 14th-century tower to serve as a reminder of the bustling period of Bruges's greatness. There is the alternative, in which Belgian men of letters have found matter for poignant reflection, between admiring the monuments produced by an age of vigorous action, an incitement, as Verhaeren has implied, to a renewed life and energy and on the other hand the mood in which Georges Rodenbach contemplates *Bruges la Morte* as a city that has died and become a shrine, where the sound of bells, the unworldly routine of the Béguinage and the vista of calm and empty waters invite only spiritual meditation (see plate 90).

It is possible to be moved by both sentiments. In the original foreport of Bruges, now the sleeping village of Damme, one may muse on an importance never to be restored and the distant dream of pageantry evoked by the tower of the church where the marriages of Burgundian Dukes were solemnized (see plate 5). One may feel at the same time a quickening of interest in the redevelopment of Bruges as a port by the Zeebrugge canal, with its promise for the future. Yet how fascinating it is that so much of the past has been preserved.

The elegance of the Hôtel de Ville remains (see plate 9), although the forty-eight statues of the façade were destroyed or removed during the incursions of the French at the time of the Revolution, to be replaced in the 19th century by substitute carvings of biblical figures and images of the Counts and Countesses of Flanders. The interior, though much restored has the magnificent Gothic roof of the early 15th century attributed to the master-craftsman, Jean de Valenciennes, with stone corbels carved with symbols of the seasons and pendentives with Old Testament themes (see plate 41). The effect of the Grande Salle is not greatly disturbed by the addition of wall-paintings in the 1890s, panoramic in survey of Flemish history and heraldic with the coats of arms of cities and guilds. Many are the remains of the great late-Gothic period. The work of one of its principal architectural designers, Jan van de Poele, has been traced in the beautiful octagon of the Belfry's upper stage and is to be seen in the façade of the Palais du Franc, the old administrative centre of the region outside the walls (the surviving court-room of which has Blondeel's chimney-piece). It is one of the pleasures Bruges has to give to come upon the many exquisite details of flamboyant tracery that bear witness to the final richness of Gothic architecture, domestic as well as of the church, appearing just as the early masters painted them with so much affection, in such works as are still at Bruges, in the Musée Communal and the Memlinc Museum of the Hospital of St John (see plates 2 & 51).

Restoration and conversion to new use has somewhat altered but not destroyed the impressiveness of a number of buildings of the great period; such as the old record office, or Maison de l'Ancien Greffe in that concentration of lovely architecture, the Place du Bourg, the 15th-century customs house converted into a municipal library and especially the principal surviving mansion of the past, the Hôtel Gruuthuse. The abode of Louis de Bruges, Seigneur de la Groothuuse, where he entertained Edward IV and Richard Crookback and brought together the great library that now forms part of the Bibliothèque Nationale, Paris, was aptly converted into a museum of the applied arts, including a fine collection of lace. Its original kitchen is a massive museum-piece in itself.

Yet an essential ingredient of the charm of Bruges is provided by buildings subsequent in date to the troubles of the 16th century. Their unpretentious simplicity is, as it were, timelessly ancient. Many of the picturesque houses lining the canals belong to the 17th century. Though the Béguinage was founded in medieval times and its lay sisterhood wears the wimple and black gown that Memlinc and David painted, the tranquil, monastic atmosphere of its buildings is largely due to the 17th and 18th centuries. If the city has 'died' in an economic and commercial sense, it has preserved in such an institution the idea of a dedicated life and with it the deep-rooted religious tradition that has its spectacular vent in the Maytime ceremony and procession when the shrine of the Holy Blood is borne through the streets.

Separated only by some thirty miles, Ghent and Bruges had a relation in the past in some ways like that of Florence and Siena. There is a parallel in their development but also a marked difference of character. They shared the prosperity of the later Middle Ages. It has been calculated that out of 50,000 inhabitants at Ghent in the 15th century 4,000 were employed in the weaving industry. But the independent and democratic spirit was stronger there than at Bruges, the cause of frequent turmoil and also of vigorous initiative. Ghent was never resigned to imposed authority, political or religious, nor did it resign itself to the decay that has preserved the medieval aspect of Bruges. When the weaving industry declined, the carrying trade along its many waterways was a new source of prosperity. Later developments were the linen and cotton industries. The modern Ghent, a port with its separate access to the mouth of the Scheldt, the centre of a network of water-borne traffic, of textile production, celebrated also for horticulture and its great flower shows, is a city that lives fully in the 20th century.

Even so there are great relics of the past and suggestions of its turbulent and heroic character. The Castle of the Counts remains (see plate 1) the most magnificent

87   Corner of the Hôtel de Ville and old Guild Houses, Grand'Place, Brussels.

88   The courtyard of Rubens's House in Antwerp.

Romanesque stronghold in Europe, without trace now of the 19th-century disrespect that turned it for a time into a cotton mill. *Son et lumière* have vividly evoked the festivities of the vast banqueting hall, the terrors of the dungeon and torture chamber, the excitement of defence on the battlemented circumference. Flickering lights and ghostly voices might recall the scene when in 1339, Jacob van Artevelde, the powerful 'Brewer of Ghent' entertained Edward III of England and concerted the deal to maintain trade between Flanders and England during the Hundred Years War. The shouts and flurry of footsteps along the battlements and at the watch-towers could bring to mind many an occasion of civic riot and popular defiance.

The Belfry, its spire still surmounted by the gilt dragon captured from Bruges, its clock-tower containing a 52-bell carillon, rises to the imposing height which the look-out over the Flanders plain required in the 14th century, though planned originally to be 100 feet higher still. It is one feature of a remarkable group or succession of buildings, together with the Romanesque bulk of the church of St Nicolas (see plate 44) and the 15th-century tower of the cathedral church of St Bavon (see plate 45); impressive as seen soaring above the surrounding gables from the flat roof of the Castle, or in related variety of turrets and spires from St Michael's Bridge.

Secular architecture has its story to tell of Ghent's chequered history. The Hôtel de Ville is in two different styles. It was intended to rival Brussels and Louvain in splendour when it was begun in 1518 at a time when Ghent still enjoyed high favour with the young Emperor Charles V who was born there at the (no longer extant) Prinsenhof palace in 1500. The façade first completed is a fine example of the ornate Gothic of the early 16th century (see plate 10). But when the revolt of 1539 against Charles's taxation was crushed and Ghent was stripped of all its civic privileges, the work was halted. The religious conflicts of the century hindered its resumption. It was completed in the Renaissance style after an interval of a hundred years.

The decline of the traditional weaving industry is signalized by Ghent's 15th-century Cloth Hall, one of the last buildings of its kind, constructed at the foot of the belfry but left unfinished as no longer of use. By 1613 it had become a fencing school for the *Serment des Escrimeurs*. It was left to the 20th century to finish its structure and turn it into a place of entertainment. On the other hand the emergence of new and prosperous trading corporations, mainly concerned with the river transport of grain, has its evidence in the picturesque buildings that line the river Lys, in style representing the transition from Gothic to Renaissance. The Quai aux Herbes (see plate 4) has among its delightful façades a characteristic example in the House of the Free Boatmen (*Francs Bateliers*), its tall façade, designed by C. van den Berghe in 1531, crowned by fanciful gables and columns and decorated with low-reliefs that include the arms of Charles V and a variety of marine motifs.

Ghent has many churches but few remains of its once numerous monasteries. The ancient monastic foundation of Byloke Abbey is a pleasant museum full of memories of Ghent in times gone by. The medieval buildings of the once great abbey of St Bavon where Edward III and his Queen Philippa stayed and John of Gaunt was born comprise the lapidary museum which contains the tombstone of Hubert van Eyck, discovered during the restoration of the cathedral in 1892. The religious tradition of the Middle Ages, as at Bruges, is continued in the Little Béguinage, a whole township of the devout within high walls, where the resident sisters combine the life of prayer with the endless tasks of sewing and embroidery that support the community.

The great treasure of the religious past and the art that accompanied it is the

89　Façade of the studio and the courtyard of Rubens's House, Antwerp.

90　The Béguinage, Bruges.

'Adoration of the Lamb' in the Cathedral of St Bavon (see plates 18, 19 & 33). Works of art in the Flemish cities have several times been endangered or removed by invading forces. The masterpiece of the brothers van Eyck has survived almost intact, though only after many adventures. It escaped the iconoclasm of the 16th century when Ghent was for a time a centre of protestant revolt. But it was carried off to Paris along with many other looted works, when the French Revolutionary forces, at war with Austria, swept into the then Austrian Netherlands. It was returned in 1816 after the defeat of Napoleon, though dismemberment was the next threat.

An unauthorized sale of side panels took them to Berlin. Those with the naked figures of Adam and Eve (which the disapproval of the Emperor Joseph II had kept shuttered from public view) were transferred to the Museum at Brussels in 1861. The altarpiece was reassembled after the First World War. In the Second World War it was part of the Nazi loot, like the Madonna and Child by Michelangelo from the church of Notre-Dame, Bruges (see plate 50). Both great works have happily been reclaimed. The triptych by Justus of Ghent in St Bavon, with its central panel of the Crucifixion, is a fine work in which the influence of both van Eyck and van der Weyden can be perceived.

The Palace of Horticulture in the Parc de la Citadelle at Ghent (on the site of the fortifications built by Charles V), the annual *Floralia* and the extensive nursery gardens of the region have their bearing on that love of flowers which has made of Flemish art an incomparable painted garden since the time of van Eyck and the masters of the illuminated manuscript who flourished at Ghent as at Bruges.

The changes of the centuries are inevitably written in the aspect of the Flemish cities. The nearness of France and the dominance of French taste in the 18th century are reflected at Ghent in the elegance of classical façades and rococo interiors, in surviving mansions such as that in the rue Jan-Breydel which is now the Museum of the Decorative Arts and the Hotel d'Hane-Steenhuyse in the rue des Champs, a medieval house entirely rebuilt in 1768. Change is still more marked at Brussels. It is surprising to think of it as once enclosed by walls begun in the 14th century, with eight gates and 127 round towers spaced at equal intervals, but they remained intact until the early 19th century. A remnant has survived in the Porte de Hal, converted into a museum of arms and armour. Much of the city's ancient beauty was destroyed in the bombardment by the French forces of the Duc de Villeroi in 1695, during the campaigns that made a complex prelude to the War of the Spanish Succession. The rain of red-hot cannon-balls is said to have demolished some 4,000 buildings and wrecked hundreds more. The Grand'Place, scene of innumerable festivals, pageants, ceremonies and open-air stage performances when the Burgundians and Habsburgs held their court at Brussels, was laid waste.

What survived, though not without damage which included the loss of paintings by van der Weyden, Rubens and van Dyck, was one of the most beautiful examples of the Flemish town hall, planned at the beginning of the 15th century to assert a civic dignity in the capital of Brabant comparable with that of Bruges (see plate 7). Its graceful tower and sculptured front remain sumptuous in effect. So too is the interior, though bearing the stamp of the 18th and 19th centuries in décor.

As rebuilt not long after the bombardment, the Guild Houses of the Grand'Place, always noted for their richness of decoration, took on that ornateness of fantasy that still astonishes and fascinates the visitor whether seen by day as the background of crowds around the gay flower stalls or with all the theatrical night effect of flood lighting (see plate 87). The architects, de Bruyn and Pastorama vied in the pomp they bestowed on the buildings, described by the names of inns and mansions of an earlier date than the guilds themselves; the 'Cornet', house of the boatmen, with a gable in the shape of a frigate, accompanied by seahorses and tritons and with

Fig. 47 Façade of the Hôtel d'Hane Steenhuyse, Ghent.

cannon at the embrasures represented by the windows; the 'Fox', house of the mercers, lavishly adorned with sculpture by Marc de Vos (see fig. 51); the 'She-Wolf' of the archers, crowned by a phoenix; the 'Sack' of the cabinet-makers; the 'Wheelbarrow' of the chandlers; the bakers' hall with golded dome. The grandiose structure on the East, the 'House of the Dukes of Brabant' by de Bruyn, accommodated several guilds. The profusion of columns, reliefs, statues and caryatids and cartouches is unique in flamboyance. Opposite the Hôtel de Ville, the 'Maison du Roi', now the city museum, is a careful reconstruction of the 1870s of a building, the one-time Breadhouse, originally in the richly decorated Gothic style of the late 15th century. More of the old Brussels was destroyed in the 19th century when the river Senne was dredged and covered over – the aspect of the old quarters is recorded in the paintings by J. B. van Moer in the burgomaster's antechamber of the Hôtel de Ville. There remain as elsewhere those lasting monuments of the Gothic age, the churches; the cathedral of St Gudule (see plate 42), Notre-Dame au Sablon (see plates 43 & 48), Notre-Dame de la Chapelle (which contains the tomb of Pieter Brueghel the Elder, erected by his son, Jan). But a general view of Brussels is of a capital of formal neo-classicism in palaces and public buildings and with all the later evidences of modern progress. A remaining classical enclave in the centre of the city, generally dominated today by vast late 19th-century buildings, is the quiet and restrained *Place des Martyres,* a severe northern version of the Louis Seize style. The neo-classic sobriety is in contrast with the humour of the city mascot, the Manneken Pis, adapted possibly by the 17th-century sculptor du Quesnoy from a fountain design by Correggio.

Fig. 48 Maison du Roi, Brussels.

Brussels is a city of art in the special sense of a city of art museums. The Albert I Library houses the great collection of manuscripts that reflects the taste of the Dukes of Burgundy. The great masters of Flemish painting from the 15th to the 17th century are a magnificent array in the Musées Royaux des Beaux Arts. The Palais du Cinquantenaire, an exhibition building of 1880, contains the museum of decorative and industrial art, an historic record of craftsmanship, rich in examples of lace, tapestry, goldsmith work and carving. There is that *tour de force* of the lace-maker's art and craft, the bedspread presented to Archduke Albert and Isabella in 1599 on their marriage (see front end-paper) with its 120 minutely worked historical scenes; such master works of the Brussels *tapissier* as the 'Legend of Notre-Dame au Sablon' and 'Master Philip's Deposition' of the early 16th century; such a beautiful example of medieval goldsmith work in the Meuse region as the reliquary cross in delicate filigree by Brother Hugo of St Marie d'Oignies; such Gothic virtuosity in woodcarving as Jan Borman's altarpiece of the martyrdom of St George (see plate 52).

As a great port, restored and immensely expanded since the Second World War, Antwerp with its mile upon mile of docks, cranes, warehouses, its maze of waterways and incessant movement of marine traffic seems to leave the past the farther behind, to emphasize the more emphatically its difference from dreaming Bruges. There are scant reminders of a medieval Antwerp. The Steen is a solitary fragment of its ancient castle, much restored and turned into a museum of antiquities. But the energy characteristic of the city is to be found in what remains of the 16th and 17th centuries. It appears in the exuberance of the cathedral's great north tower soaring to its height of 400 feet (see plate 6); in all the evidences the city preserves of Rubens's dynamic presence and powers. In addition to the great works in Antwerp's churches and museum there is his house as restored to recall the patrician state in which he lived, the studio whence so many masterpieces came (see plates 88 & 89).

Restoration and reconstruction as in other Flemish cities preserve the memory of the past. The arcades of the Bourse, built on the site of the building that reflected Antwerp's financial and commercial eminence in the early 16th century, keep as much of the late-Gothic character due originally to Dominicus de Waghemakere as J. Schadde could provide in the 1860s. The Hôtel de Ville conserves externally the Renaissance aspect that Cornelis de Vriendt gave it in the 1560s, its long façade dominated centrally by the lofty and richly decorated and gabled pavilion, more exuberantly Flemish than the rest. The interior, pillaged in the fury of 1576 but rehabilitated in 1581, was again restored in the latter half of the 19th century, and adorned with memories of past greatness by the Belgian school of patriotic history painters. Hendrik Leys (1815–69), revered in his time as a national figure, a Quinten Metsys reborn, expressed his romantic yearning towards the time and spirit of the old Flemish masters in the paintings of Charles V's state entry into Antwerp, and scenes representing municipal rights and defence in the 16th century. A like homage to the past appears in the profusion of patriotically inspired sculpture in 19th-century Belgium.

Various phases of restoration have not destroyed the Renaissance harmony of the guild houses in the Grand'Place. The magnificence of a late-Gothic hall remains in the *Vieille Boucherie*, adjacent to the Quai van Dyck, built as a meat-market at the beginning of the 16th century by the senior de Waghemakere, Herman, and now converted into a museum of decorative art, containing among other things, varied examples of historic interior décor (see plate 13). The flamboyant, wrought-iron canopy of the 'Metsys' well-head in the *Marché aux Gants* is a reminder of the Flemish skill in metalwork (see plate 56) and, if tradition be trusted, of Metsys' own design.

Though the cathedral has suffered at different times from fire, iconoclasm

91 Detail from 'The Census at Bethlehem' by Pieter Brueghel. (Whole painting 44½ × 64½in., 113 × 163cm.) *Brussels, Musée des Beaux Arts.*

92 Detail from the tapestry cycle 'History of Jacob' by Bernard van Orley. *Brussels, Musée d'Art et d'Histoire.*

93 Detail from the tapestry cycle 'History of Jacob' by Bernard van Orley. *Brussels, Musée d'Art et d'Histoire.*

94 'The King Drinks' by Jacob Jordaens, c. 1638. (62⅜ × 84in., 56 × 210cm.) *Brussels, Musée d'Art Ancien.*

Fig. 49   Rubens's House at Antwerp, 1684, by Frans Harrewijn (after J. van Croes). *London, British Museum.*

and the pillage of invaders, the interior as well as the great north tower are vastly impressive in their proportions as are also the important works of Rubens it contains. The church of St Jacques, built in several phases from 1491 to 1694 and showing an architectural transition from late-Gothic to baroque, comes next in importance to the cathedral by reason of its rich decoration, though it was damaged by a fire in 1968. The chapel with the tombs of the Rubens family contained the 'Madonna and Saints' painted during the great artist's last years, with the figure of St George bearing a banner, once popularly believed (but without foundation) to portray Rubens himself.

The Jesuit church on which he lavished his decorative art was destroyed by fire in the early 18th century but rebuilt later in the same style. The three altarpieces by Rubens, the Assumption and the Miracles of St Ignatius Loyola and St Francis Xavier, fortunately salvaged, are now in the Kunsthistorisches Museum, Vienna. The church of St Augustine, however, built 1615–18, retains the intensely dramatic 'Betrothal of St Catherine' painted in 1628, at about the same time as van Dyck and Jordaens also made their contribution of paintings to the interior.

A vivid memory of achievement is given by the Plantin-Moretus Museum in the premises of the historic printing-house themselves, a rare and beautiful example of the Flemish domestication of the Renaissance style. The remarkable dynasty of printers had continued to operate there until in 1876 the city of Antwerp acquired the building and its contents. The composing and printing rooms of 1579, the proof-readers' room, the type foundry, the first editions, the specimens of printing and engraving, the family portraits, the souvenirs of association with Rubens and other artists make up a unique record of the printing industry.

In the Antwerp Musée des Beaux Arts, the pictures that came from the Guild of St Luke when it ceased to operate, from suppressed religious foundations and from churches and other sources, present a panorama of Flemish painting from van Eyck and van der Weyden to Rubens and van Dyck. Although great works by the Flemish masters are now widely distributed in the world's galleries, the cities in which they were produced and which fostered their production, retain as Antwerp does, and Bruges and Brussels also, a magnificent residuum and heritage.

Fig. 50   Courtyard, Plantin-Moretus Museum, Antwerp.

Fig. 51   Artisan putti. Relief over doorway of Guildhouse. Grand'Place, Brussels.

95   Detail from 'The Garden of Love' by Rubens, c. 1620. (Whole painting $79\frac{1}{4} \times 113\frac{1}{4}$in., 198×283cm.) *Madrid, Museo del Prado*.

96   'Rubens and his first wife Isabella Brant' by Rubens, 1609. ($27\frac{1}{2} \times 20\frac{1}{2}$in., $68\cdot5 \times 52$cm.) *Munich, Altepinakothek*.

97   Detail from 'La Kermesse' by Rubens, c. 1636. (Whole painting 59×102in., 198×283cm.) *Paris, Musée du Louvre*.

I The Franco-Flemish School, 14th–15th century

PIERRE of Brussels, JEAN of Ghent, EVRARD of Hainault. Flemish miniaturists working in France, late 14th century.

JEAN of Bruges. 14th-century miniaturist, designer of tapestry.

JACQUES COENE. Architect, painter and miniaturist, active at end of the 14th century. Illustrator of a Bible for Philip the Bold.

POL, JEANNEQUIN, HERMAN of Limbourg. 14th–15th-century miniaturists. Worked for Philip the Bold and Duc de Berry. Their principal work the *Très Riches Heures du Duc de Berry* (Musée Condé, Chantilly).

ANDRE BEAUNEVEU. 14th-century miniaturist and sculptor of Valenciennes.

JEAN MALOUEL. 14th-century painter, born in Gelderland, who worked at Dijon for Philip the Bold.

HENRI BELLECHOSE. Brabant painter of the early 15th century who worked at Dijon in succession to Malouel.

MELCHIOR BROEDERLAM of Ypres. Active at end of 14th century, painter of altarpiece for the Chartreuse of Champmol (now in the Dijon Museum).

II The Rise of Netherlandish Painting, 15th–16th century

Bruges

VAN EYCK. The brothers, Hubert and Jan. Jan (*c.* 1390–1441) born at Maaseyck, more closely identified with Bruges. Both are supposed to have collaborated in the great 'Adoration of the Lamb' (Ghent). Jan worked for Philip the Good.

PETRUS CHRISTUS (*c.* 1410–72). Born at Baerle, settled at Bruges where he followed Jan van Eyck.

HANS MEMLINC (*c.* 1435–94). Born at Seligenstadt near Mainz he came to Flanders as a young man and settled at Bruges after 1465, working there for the rest of his life.

GERARD DAVID (*c.* 1460–1513). Born at Oudewater, near Gouda, came to Bruges in 1483.

JAN PROVOOST (or PROVOST) (1462–1529). Born at Mons, trained at Valenciennes, settled at Bruges after 1483.

AMBROSIUS BENSON (d. *c.* 1550). Native of Lombardy, recorded master at Bruges in 1519.

ADRIAEN YSENBRANDT (*c.* 1425–1551). Native of Haarlem, at Bruges from 1510, a follower of David.

Brussels

ROGER VAN DER WEYDEN (*c.* 1399–1464). Born at Tournai, pupil of Robert Campin, from 1432 painter at Brussels.

THE MASTER OF FLEMALLE. Identified with ROBERT CAMPIN (*c.* 1378–1444) who worked at Tournai and was the master of van der Weyden.

DIRCK (or THIERRY) BOUTS (*c.* 1460–1549). Born at Haarlem probably trained at Brussels with van der Weyden, worked at Louvain.

Ghent

HUGO VAN DER GOES (*c.* 1440–82). A master at Ghent in 1467, devised decorations for the marriage of Charles the Bold and Margaret of York, later retired to the Rouge-Cloître monastery.

JOOS VAN WASSENHOVE (Justus van Ghent). Probably born at Ghent, a friend of van der Goes. He worked in Italy from 1473.

III Developments of the 16th century

The influence of Italian art appears in the work both of Dutch artists established in Holland, e.g. CORNELISZ VAN OOSTSANEN (Amsterdam), JAN SCOREL (Utrecht), MARTIN VAN HEEMSKERCK (Haarlem, Utrecht); and of artists working in the southern provinces of the Netherlands.

Antwerp

JAN GOSSAERT (MABUSE) (*c.* 1475–1533). Born at (?) Maubeuge, a master at Antwerp, influenced by Italian Renaissance art.

QUINTEN METSYS (or MASSYS) (1466–1530). Born at Louvain, settled at Antwerp, 1491. Painter of varied output, showing both Flemish and north Italian influence.

JOOS VAN CLEVE (1491–1540). Master at Antwerp, 1511, travelled in Italy and worked at several European courts.

Brussels

BERNARD VAN ORLEY (1488–1541). Born at Brussels, painter and designer of tapestry and stained-glass, employed by the regent, Margaret of Austria.

GILLIS VAN CONINXLOO (1544–1607). Born at Antwerp, worked at Brussels, noted for his landscapes.

The following artists are more specifically described as 'Romanists'

PIETER COECKE (1502–50). Painter and designer, born at Alost, pupil of van Orley, worked in Rome and translated Italian treatises on architecture.

LAMBERT LOMBARD (*c.* 1506–66). Born at Liège, architect, painter and engraver. Influenced by visit to Rome, 1537.

FRANS DE VRIENDT (FLORIS) (1516–70). Painter and sculptor, born at Antwerp, pupil of Lambert Lombard, master at Antwerp, 1540. Went to Italy with his brother, the architect and sculptor, Cornelis de Vriendt.

PIETER POURBUS (*c.* 1510–84). Born at Gouda, worked at Bruges.

OTTO VAN VEEN (1566–1629). Born at Leyden, worked at Liège, Brussels and Antwerp, and in Rome; was influenced by Venetian painting.

ADAM VAN NOORT (1562–1641). Born at Antwerp, influenced in Italy by the Venetians.

Other Romanists were BARTHEL SPRANGER (*c.* 1646–*c.* 1627), the brothers, AMBROSE, FRANS and JEROME FRANCKEN (active end of 16th century), DENIS CALVAERT (1540–1619), MICHIEL COXCIE (1499–1592).

The development of various secular themes was a feature of the period: Portraiture

ANTHONIS MOR (1512–75). Born at Utrecht, pupil of Jan Scorel, master at Antwerp, 1547. Visited Rome, portrait painter at Lisbon, Madrid and London.

WILLEM and ADRIAEN THOMASZ KEY. Uncle and nephew, active at Antwerp in the 16th century.

MARTEN DE VOS (*c.* 1531–1603). Born at Antwerp, pupil of Frans Floris. Painter of portraits and religious subjects.

Genre

JEROME BOSCH (HIERONYMUS VAN AKEN) (active late 15th century, d. 1516). Born and worked at 's-Hertogenbosch (Bois-le-Duc), north Brabant, a unique figure in religious, fantastic and satirical art.

MARINUS VAN REYMERSWAEL (16th century). Born in Zeeland, settled in 1509 at Antwerp, satirical painter of the 'money lender and wife' theme.

PIETER AERTSEN (1507–75). Born at Amsterdam, master at Antwerp, 1535, painter of market and domestic subjects.

JOACHIM BEUCKELAER (c. 1533–73). Born at Antwerp, follower of Aertsen.

PIETER BRUEGHEL the Elder (c. 1525–69). Born at Breugel (Brabant), pupil of Pieter Coecke at Antwerp, influenced by Bosch in satirical and allegorical themes, but eminent in scenes of everyday life and landscape. Worked at Antwerp and Brussels. His eldest son Pieter Brueghel the Younger (c. 1564–1637), born at Brussels, followed him in subject-matter.

Landscape

JEROME COCK (c. 1510–70). Born at Antwerp, painter and engraver for whom Pieter Brueghel the Elder worked, c. 1550.

JOACHIM PATINIR (c. 1480–1524). Born near Dinant, master at Antwerp, 1515, gave landscape primary importance in subjects to which a number of collaborators added figures.

TOBIAS VERHAECHT (1561–1631). Born at Antwerp, master there in 1590. He was the first master of Rubens.

ROELANDT SAVERY (1576–1639). Born at Courtrai, worked at Prague for the Emperor Rudolph, painted minutely detailed landscapes, animals and flowers.

Other painters of landscape were ABEL and JACOB GRIMMER (end of the 16th century), HANS BOL (1534–93), and LUCAS, MARTIN and FREDERIC VAN VALCKENBORGH (16th–17th century).

IV The Age of Rubens

PETER PAUL RUBENS (1577–1640). Born at Siegen, Westphalia, trained at Antwerp. After eight years in Italy, with an interval in Spain, and after thorough study of the Italian masters, he returned to Antwerp in 1608 to become its supreme representative in painting, greatly influencing and inspiring his Flemish contemporaries.

ANTON VAN DYCK (1599–1641). Born at Antwerp, worked in the studio of the portrait painter, Hendrik van Balen (1573–1632). Assistant for a time of Rubens but five years spent in Italy gave him an independent education in style. He painted religious and mythological subjects in the baroque manner on return to Antwerp and in 1632 became portrait painter to Charles I in England.

The circle and followers of Rubens

ABRAHAM JANSSENS (1575–1632). Born at Antwerp, studied in Italy and was influenced in religious and mythological subjects by Caravaggio and by Rubens. His pupils were Gerard Seghers (1591–1631) and Theodor Rombouts (1597–1637).

THEODOR VAN THULDEN (1606–76). Born at Bois-le-Duc, pupil of Rubens, continuing his style in religious, mythological and allegorical subjects and designs for tapestry and stained glass (e.g. in St Gudule, Brussels).

ERASMUS QUELLIN (1607–78). Born at Antwerp, son of the sculptor Erasmus Quellin and brother of the sculptor Artus, and engraver Hubert. Pupil of Rubens and official painter to the city of Antwerp after Rubens's death.

GASPAR DE CRAYER (1584–1669). Born at Antwerp, much influenced in religious and allegorical subjects by Rubens.

JACOB JORDAENS (1593–1678). Born at Antwerp, the pupil of Adam van Noort. Associated after 1631 with Rubens of whose manner he gives a robust Flemish version in allegories and scenes of contemporary life.

CORNELIS DE VOS (1585–1651). Born at Hulst in Flanders, worked at Antwerp probably as a collaborator with Rubens. Noted mainly for portraits.

Animal, Still-Life and Flower Painters

JAN ('VELVET') BRUEGHEL (1568–1625). Born at Brussels, second son of Pieter Brueghel the Elder, painter of landscapes, animals and flowers, the friend and collaborator of Rubens.

FRANS SNYDERS (1579–1657). Born at Antwerp, pupil of Pieter Brueghel II and Hendrik van Balen, after visit to Italy associated with Rubens as collaborator and friend, also collaborated with Jordaens.

PAUL DE VOS (c. 1590–1678). Brother of Cornelis de Vos, born at Hulst, worked with his brother-in-law, Snyders, as animal painter.

JAN FYT (1611–61). Painter and engraver, born at Antwerp, pupil of Snyders as animal and still-life specialist.

DANIEL SEGHERS (1590–1661). Born at Antwerp, pupil of 'Velvet' Brueghel, joined the Jesuit Order, 1614, painted floral garlands for religious subjects.

JAN VAN KESSEL the Elder (1626–79). Born at Antwerp, pupil of Simon de Vos and Jan Brueghel, painted animals, birds and still-life.

Landscape Painters

PAUL BRIL (1554–1626). Born at Antwerp, painter and engraver, worked in Rome with his brother Matheus (1550–84), also a landscape painter.

FRANS WOUTERS (1612–59). Born at Lierre, pupil of Rubens, master at Antwerp, 1634, worked in Germany and England.

Also LUCAS VAN UDEN (1595–1672), worked with Rubens at Antwerp; JACQUES FOUQUIERES (1580–1659), pupil of Jan Brueghel, also worked with Rubens.

JACOB VAN ARTHOIS (1613–86). Born at Brussels, painted landscapes for the subjects of other artists, specialized in views of the forest of Soignies. CORNELIS HUYSMANS (1647–1727). Born at Antwerp, pupil of van Arthois. PEETERS family, views of Antwerp.

Genre Painters

ADRIAEN BROUWER (1605–38). Born at Audenarde, worked at Haarlem, master at Antwerp, 1631. Influenced JOOS VAN CRAESBEEK (1606–54).

DAVID TENIERS the Younger (1610–90). Born at Antwerp, pupil of his father, much influenced by Brouwer, court painter at Brussels to the Archduke Leopold, 1651.

GONZALES COQUES (1614–84). Born at Antwerp, pupil of Pieter Brueghel the Younger, master at Antwerp in 1641, painter of portraits and genre known as 'the little van Dyck'.

PIETER SNAYERS (1592–1667). Born at Antwerp, pupil of Sebastian Vranckx (1573–1647), painter of battle scenes and landscapes.

JAN SIBERECHTS (1627–c. 1703). Born at Antwerp where he worked until 1672, then in England, painter of rustic scenes.

Bibliography

An informative general survey of land, people, cities and art is *The Treasure-House of Belgium*, E. Cammaerts, 1924. The evolution of characteristic forms of civic architecture is described in detail in *Beffrois, Halles, Hôtels de Ville dans le Nord de la France et la Belgique*, M. Battard, 1948. Architectural references include M. Nijhoff, *La Belgique Monumentale*, 1915 and K. Sluyterman, *Ancient Interiors in Belgium*, 1915. Impressions of famous travellers in the past are L. Guicciardini, *Description of the Low-Countries* (1567 – Eng. trans. 1920) and G. Marlier and J. A. Goris (editors), Albert Dürer, *Journal de voyage dans les Pays-Bas*, 1937.

Among topographical and historical studies are T. Edwards, *Belgium and Luxembourg*, 1951; W. H. J. Weale, *Bruges et ses environs*, 1884; Gilliat-Smith, *The Story of Bruges*, 1910; H. Hymans, *Bruges et Ypres; Gand et Tournai; Bruxelles*, 1910; A. Génard, *Anvers à travers les ages;* Max Rooses, *The Plantin-Moretus Museum, Antwerp*.

The literature of Flemish pictorial art is vast. Flemish painting of the 15th century is generally described in J. van der Elst, *The Last Flowering of the Middle Ages*, 1945. Works on miniature painting include P. Durrieu, *La miniature flamande au temps de la Cour de Bourgogne*, 1921; L. M. J. Delaissé, *La Miniature flamande à l'époque de Philippe le Bon*, 1956; *Miniatures Médiévales de la Librairie de Bourgogne*, 1959.

Histories and studies of painting include M. Friedlander, *Die Altniederländische Malerei*, 14 vols. 1924–37; *From van Eyck to Bruegel*, 1956; L. Puyvelde, *The Flemish Primitives*, 1948; E. Panofsky, *Early Netherlandish Painting*, 1953; R. H. Wilenski, *Flemish Painters, 1430–1830*, 2 vols. 1960; L. Maeterlinck, *Le genre satirique dans la peinture flamande*, 1907; P. Fierens, *La fantastique dans l'art flamand*, 1947; F. Griendl, *Les peintres flamands de nature morte au XVIIe siècle*, 1956; M. L. Hairs, *Les peintres flamands de fleurs au XVIIe siècle*, 1955.

Among works on individual masters are Weale and Brockwell, *The van Eycks and their Art*, 1912; W. H. J. Weale, *Hans Memlinc*, 1901, *Gerard David*, 1895; J. Destrée, *H. van der Goes*, 1914; *R. van der Weyden*, 1930; C. de Tolnay, *Le Maître de Flémalle*, 1938; *Bosch*, 1937; R. L. Delevoy, *Bosch*, 1960; R. van Bastelaer and G. H. de Loo, *P. Brueghel*, 1907; F. Grossmann, *Bruegel, the Paintings*, 1954; L. Munz, *Bruegel, the Drawings*, 1961; J. Burckhardt, *Rubens* (Eng. trans. 1950); Max Rooses, *L'Oeuvre de P. P. Rubens*, 5 vols, 1886–92; L. Cust, *A. van Dyck*, 1900; L. Burchard and R. A. d'Hulst, *Rubens Drawings*, 1963.

Works on sculpture and craft include J. de Borchgrave d'Altena, *Oeuvres de nos Imagiers Romans et Gothiques*, 1944; E. Marchal, *La sculpture et les chefs d'oeuvres de l'orfevrerie belge*, 1895; H. David, *Claus Sluter*, 1951; J. Guiffrey, *La tapisserie du XIIe siècle à la fin du XVIe siècle;* J. Destrée, *Tapisseries Bruxelloises*, 1906.

The catalogues of a long series of important exhibitions are valuable references. The exhibitions include *L'Art Belge au XVIIe Siècle*, Palais du Cinquantenaire, Brussels, 1910; *L'Art ancien dans les Flandres (Région de l'Escaut)*, Ghent, 1913; *Flemish and Belgian Art*, Royal Academy, 1927. Memorial volume ed. by Sir Martin Conway; *De van Eyck à Bruegel*, Orangerie, Paris, 1935; *Flemish Art (1300–1700)*, Royal Academy, 1953–4; *Le Siècle des Primitifs Flamands*, Bruges, 1960; *Fleurs et Jardins dans l'Art Flamand*, Ghent, 1960.

List of figures

Index